CHAMPI★NS ★F FREED★M

GOTTFRIED DIETZE
M. STANTON EVANS
ANTONY FISHER
SHIRLEY R. LETWIN
B. A. ROGGE
ESMOND WRIGHT

CHAMPIONS OF FREEDOM

Edited by Barbara J. Smith
Hillsdale College Press • Hillsdale, Michigan • 1976

Contents

Preface

Ludwig von Mises, who died in 1973 at the age of 92, was one of our century's most prominent defenders of human liberty and a dedicated opponent of government intervention in the economy. In his many books and articles Dr. von Mises defended private property, the importance of the individual, freedom, and limited government. He successfully proved that a free society cannot exist without a free economy.

For the third year, Hillsdale College is pleased to present six distinguished lecturers who have been significantly influenced by Mises. It is appropriate that this series, which commemorates both the man and his works, takes place at Hillsdale College, for Hillsdale has one of the most thoroughly Misesian economics departments in the country. The admiration of Hillsdale College and Dr. von Mises was reciprocal. In his will he specified that Hillsdale College receive his entire personal library, which is now housed in a special room in the Mossey Library.

This is the third volume of *Champions of Freedom*, an ongoing compilation of each year's presentations in the Ludwig von Mises Lecture Series at Hillsdale College.

Notes on Contributors

Esmond Wright

Esmond Wright was educated at Durham University in England and at the University of Virginia in the United States. During World War II he spent five years in the British military service in the Middle East and ended his army career as a lieutenant colonel in Cairo. He has been a member of the British House of Commons for the Pollock Division of Glasgow.

He is now director of the Institute of United States Studies and professor of American history at the University of London. Among his books are *Washington and the American Revolution, Fabric of Freedom, Benjamin Franklin and American Independence* and *The Causes and Consequences of the American Revolution.*

M. Stanton Evans

M. Stanton Evans is a syndicated columnist for the Los Angeles Times syndicate and a commentator for the CBS radio network. Since 1971 he has served as chairman of the American Conservative Union.

A former editor of the *Indianapolis News*, Evans has served as assistant editor of *The Freeman* and managing editor of *Human Events*, and is currently a contributing editor and regular columnist for that publication.

Evans graduated from Yale in 1955 and attended New York University where he did graduate work in economics. His books include *The Liberal Establishment, Revolt on Campus, The Future of Conservatism*, and *Clear and Present Dangers*.

B. A. Rogge

Benjamin A. Rogge received his A.B. degree from Hastings College in 1940. He also holds an M.A. degree from the University of Nebraska and a Ph.D. from Northwestern University.

He joined the Wabash College faculty in 1949 as an assistant professor of economics and was named dean of the college in 1956. He served in that position until 1964 when he received his appointment as distinguished professor of political economy.

Dr. Rogge is a lecturer in the School of Banking, sponsored by the American Bankers Association at the University of Wisconsin, and is a trustee of the Foundation for Economic Education.

Gottfried Dietze

Gottfried Dietze is professor of political science at The Johns Hopkins University. He has taken the following degrees: Dr. Jur., University of Heidelberg; Ph.D., Princeton University; and S.J.D., University of Virginia.

His books in English include: *The Federalist: A Classic on Federalism and Free Government; In Defense of Property; Magna Carta and Property; America's Political Dilemma: From Limited to Unlimited Democracy;* and *Youth, University and Democracy.* Professor Dietze is also the editor of *Essays on the American Constitution.*

Antony Fisher

Born in 1915, Antony Fisher was educated at Eton and at Cambridge University. He chose to pursue farming as a fulltime occupation in 1950. Four years later, he founded the Buxted Chicken Co., which after a merger became Allied Farm Foods, the largest poultry processing company in Europe.

In 1955, Fisher founded the Institute of Economic Affairs, a research group highly respected in business and academic circles. He is also the founder of the International Institute for Economic Research, begun in 1970. Now retired from all business activities, Fisher continues to lecture extensively, especially in the U.S., on current economic problems.

He is the author of *Must History Repeat Itself?* published by the Churchill Press.

Shirley R. Letwin

Shirley R. Letwin holds the M.A. and Ph.D. degrees from the University of Chicago. While completing her doctorate, she studied under Nobel Prize-winning economist F. A. Hayek.

Currently teaching for Peterhouse, Cambridge University, she has previously taught at the London School of Economics, and at Harvard, Brandeis, and the University of Chicago.

She is the author of numerous essays, reviews, and two books: *Human Freedom* and *The Pursuit of Certainty: David Hume, Jeremy Bentham, J. S. Mill, Beatrice Webb.*

Introduction

Your president, Dr. George Roche, has invited me to come here, and first of all I want to thank him for this invitation. But specially I want to thank him for the active interest he has been taking in the promotion of Ludwig von Mises' ideas and ideals. Furthermore I want to tell him, and all of you, how much I admire him for the courage with which he attacks the most difficult problems; and in spite of all the obstacles put in his way, he will not give in. On the contrary, Hillsdale College today is considered all around the world to be a center of libertarian thought—and it is your president, Dr. Roche, who has succeeded in creating this center.

It is now more than two years since I was here with you and dedicated the library of my husband to Hillsdale College. The library has found a beautiful home here and that gave me the idea to ask Dr. Roche whether I could donate my husband's desk and chair to Hillsdale to make the library seem even more a second home of his.

I remember I told you two years ago that with the library went a piece of my heart. Being honest I must tell you that the desk and the chair mean much more to me than the books. For more than thirty years I saw Ludwig von Mises sitting at this very desk, reading, writing, studying. When I came into the room, he often did not take notice of me, and if it was not necessary, I would not talk to him, so as not to interrupt the flow of his thoughts. Usually he would be writing. Once in a while he stopped, straightened up in his chair, the ballpoint in his hand, lost in his thoughts. After a few seconds he would bend down again and continue his work. His thoughts were so clear, his knowledge so deep, every subject he treated was firmly anchored in his mind. Sometimes he would get up from his chair, walk across the room to his books, look up some reference and then go back to his work. If I did not speak, he would not even see me, so complete was his concentration.

Perhaps you may have heard that I have written a book during these last two years. It is titled *My Years with Ludwig von Mises* and will be published by Arlington House. It will be available in a few months.* This book is not a scholarly book, because I am not an economist. Of course, I do talk about his work, since his work was part of our life; but mainly I have told the personal, human story of a great scholar, whose private life and struggles were not known to the admirers of his great intellect.

At around the same time another book will be published, a book my husband wrote in 1940 when we first came to this country and were not yet settled. It is written in

*January, 1977.

longhand, in German. I have typed it and sent a copy of the German manuscript to Professor Friedrich von Hayek. He wrote to me immediately that he was so fascinated he could not stop reading it, in spite of all the urgent work he had to do. He feels that this book is such an important piece of history that it should be published immediately, word for word, unedited, untouched. Professor Hans Sennholz, a former student of my late husband and a great economist in his own right——you all most probably know him——is almost through with translating the manuscript into English. Our very dear friend, Mr. Frederick Nymeyer, one of the greatest admirers of Ludwig von Mises, is going to publish it for the Libertarian Press in South Holland, Illinois. I know my husband would have been very pleased about it, because he thought very highly of Mr. Nymeyer. As it happens, Mr. Nymeyer is here in the audience tonight and I would like you all to meet him.

I have something more to tell you. About a year ago I had to arrange all the files, scripts, correspondence, and posthumous writings of my husband. At that occasion I had to open the desk and go through everything, to see what had to be filed. Then . . . something strange occurred. In the thirty-five years I was married to Ludwig von Mises, I had written many letters to him, for in the first years of our marriage I was not always with him, when he went on a lecture or a conference trip. And I myself went some-times to Paris, London, or Caracas to see my children. Then I always wrote to him, for he expected to hear from me every day. And he kept these letters, I know that very well . . . he kept them all together in one place. But when I went through the closets with his writings, I could not find anything ... not a single letter. He must have burned or torn up everything. When you have read my book *My Years with Ludwig von Mises* you will understand that I knew immediately the meaning of this act. So I was not astonished. But when I emptied the last drawer of his desk, I saw in the back of it a little wallet. I opened it and there I found an envelope with my handwriting on it and the postmark Vienna, March 1935. I had mailed this envelope to him in Geneva, where he at that time was teaching at the Graduate Institute of International Studies. I was then living in Vienna, working for a publisher, doing adaptations from English and French for the German stage. This envelope contained no letter, just a theater program and a clipping, a review about a play by the famous French author Sardou, whose play, *Dora*, I had adapted for the German stage and titled it *Diplomacy and Love*. It was produced at the Akademietheater in Vienna, which is part of the Burgtheater. The critic loved the play and at the end of his review he wrote some favorable words about me, the translator. This of course—and my name at the head of the theater program—were the reasons I had sent this envelope to him to Geneva ... that was the one memento I found.

But the little black wallet contained a second piece with my handwriting on it. I cannot make out the date, but it must have been around 1967. I had then given my husband two tickets, each worth one dollar, for the New York State lottery. He of course never believed in lotteries, but I ... I hoped for good luck. On the envelope that contained the tickets, I had written four words: "Good luck, Lu darling." These are the only words of mine written to my husband in thirty-five years of marriage that still exist. Whether my husband overlooked them or whether he wanted to keep just a small token . . . this question will not be answered.

It is my sincere wish that these mementos remain in the drawer of the desk where my husband kept them. I am happy to be able to present them to you today, together with the desk and the chair.

If I may be allowed another wish, may I hope that whatever the course of time and events, this desk and chair will be kept together with the library of Ludwig von Mises as a complete unit and memorial.

And now I want to thank you all who are here in this audience for your interest in my husband's ideas. I hope you all will go on studying Ludwig von Mises' great work and I wish you all will become successful fighters for free enterprise and human freedom—like your president, Dr. George Roche.

Margit von Mises
Hillsdale College
March, 1976

Esmond Wright

Life, Liberty, and the Pursuit of Excellence

I come before you as a symbol of a changing Britain. I was a soldier in World War II, for ten years a professor in Glasgow, for four years a member of Parliament, and since 1971 a professor again, in London—in and out of public life for more than twenty-five years. In that quarter century, as a country, Britain, unlike yourselves, has not been involved in a major war. For that we can be grateful; in our history such peaceful interludes are rare—indeed two of our wars were with yourselves. On that the less said the better. But in every other aspect of life we are passing through a social revolution.

The Empire has become the Commonwealth, and our own role in it, whatever its name, has declined. We are no longer a political island but are part of the main, a member of the European Economic Community. And at home massive social changes have taken place, which could be summarized as the decimalization and devaluation of the currency; a steady devolution of the powers of government

1

with the development of large local and the imminence of large regional assemblies; and, worst of all, demoralization, as taxation bites ever more deeply and as inflation erodes the buying power of the pound and of the pension. This is in part the result of fiscal and legislative changes due to a Labour government, but it is also the result of massive and even deeper forces than those caused by Parliament.

We are at the end of the feudal era in Britain, the age of fetlock and forelock, of the squire in the big house and the peasant at the gate, of "my station and its duties." In any case, only three out of every hundred of our people now work on the land. One in two of us lives in fact in eight big towns: London, Birmingham, Manchester, Liverpool, Leeds–Bradford, Tyneside, South Wales, and Glasgow; and indeed one in three of all the people of Scotland live within ten miles of Sauchiehall Street. Ours is a closely bound, intercity society linked by motorways and fast trains—perhaps your own Amtrak has still something to learn from us here—small, integrated, vulnerable.

Vulnerable military—No longer perhaps politically alone, but still surrounded by water, dependent for its peace and security on the sea and on the air, and to whom isolation no longer spells anything very splendid.

Vulnerable in its economy—50 percent of our food and raw materials are imported, and the sea that is our moat has also been the avenue to our marketplaces.

Vulnerable psychologically—Since the leaders of some of our former colonies, now happily independent, can at times make headlines, ensure their own local publicity, and cause us a lot of emotional and economic worry by twisting the old lion's tail. And this is true of Dominic Mintoff in

Malta, of Archbishop Makarios in Cyprus, of General Amin in Uganda, just as it used to be of Gandhi, Nehru, and Kenyatta in the past. This is part of the white man's burden. As you know as well as we do, in foreign policy even more than in domestic, there is little place for gratitude in politics.

Vulnerable socially—A prey to anxiety, worry, and economic neurosis, and worried in particular over inflation and the threat it breeds to stability. When the city of London sneezes, Manchester and Glasgow get chills. And in our integrated society when New York or Washington sneezes, Manchester and Glasgow can catch pneumonia.

To this add the problems of the Third World, the new super-power building up in China and the sense of turmoil in the Middle East. We live, to use a cliché, in revolutionary times. It is the end of the Deferential Society—at home and abroad. Its watchwords are not "deference" but "defiance" and "denial."

Perhaps the most dramatic change of all has come in the British Conservative Party. It is now led by a glamorous lady, but she was a grocer's daughter and went to Oxford on a scholarship—as did her predecessor, Ted Heath.

But then Robert Peel was a manufacturer's son, Stanley Baldwin was the son of an ironmaster, and Neville Chamberlain's family made its mark in steel and nails. Harold Macmillan was the son of a publisher. Some of these figures, including Disraeli and Churchill, never got to Oxford at all. The Conservative Party, in other words, has always produced by the most diverse systems of election and selection some very diverse leaders. In today's world they have to come from the House of Commons and by the choice of the House of Commons.

I believe profoundly that especially in a world of change, no statement of doctrine or dogma and no revolutionary logic will be permanently binding. Things always work out differently from the blueprints on the desk, from the text-book, from the prophet's view as he writes his great trea-tises in the British Museum. The art and science of govern-ment cannot be reduced to phrases or to words like social-ism, liberalism, and laissez-faire. Nor does a Conservative believe that the power of politics to put things right is unlimited. It is not only that the means are restricted but that men and women are all imperfect characters with a capacity for evil and a propensity to error, that are quite as striking as their potential for good. I am therefore averse to slogans and catch words, to talk of ideal states of society, to talk of new orders or classless dreams. None of them ever work out as their visionary idealists hoped. All of them become the instruments of wicked men. We have to live in a real world. For a Conservative everything depends on circumstances, on events and on judgments made about people. What we can do is to state not theories but convic-tions, and offer a creed rather than a decalogue. Having offered it, it is then our task to try to translate it into effect for our own times, in our own countries, in our own stage of history—as did Peel, as did Disraeli, as did Harold Macmillan. As to the future, all that we know about that is that it will be different from the past.

The truth, of course, is that democratic socialism is really a system of government which only makes any sense at all in a society which is already functioning smoothly and well, since it has to assume so many utopian condi-tions: the presence of a prestigious government, of an incorruptible and loyal bureaucracy, of a cooperative people, of a spirit of patriotism and loyalty among all classes, and of the absence of subversive groups determined to misuse the power of the state for sectional purposes.

One has only to mention these conditions to see how totally unsuitable the noble ideal of democratic socialism is to our present needs—a halo without a head to support it.

A Conservative, in other words, denies the relevance of utopias, of what Edmund Burke called abstractions and universals. As he put it, "Prudence is always the first of the political virtues." The Conservative will be the defender of the common ground and of the past inheritance. He believes that if it is not necessary to change, it is necessary not to change. Change of front, yes, as circumstances compel him. Change of ground, no. Conservatives stand on the middle way and on the common ground. They fought liberalism in the 1900s when it campaigned for total personal liberty; Conservatives then felt that it was essential to emphasize the authority and control of the state, and indeed to strengthen it where liberty for some came to mean hardship for others. So that a Tory, Lord Shaftesbury, passed the Factory Acts just as a Tory, William Wilberforce, had fought to control and abolish slavery.

Today, in fighting socialism and emphasizing freedom, Conservatives have changed their front to meet a new danger but not the ground they are defending. They see no inconsistency in opposing liberals in the name of authority and Socialists in the name of freedom. For them politics is always a matter of judgment and of balance. The Conservative stands for modesty and for moderation. He is adaptable to change because he is aware of the complexity of human nature. He is aware also of its wish for answers, of its hunger for honesty and integrity, of its dreams of greatness, of its perennial call for leadership.

I stand before you then, clothed I hope in modesty, moderation, and reasonableness. This is more important today when we constantly have to persuade and to convert. Politics is much more hampered than it used to be when the watchwords came easily, when the people voted largely from habit, and all the world seemed settled in its ways and in its innocence. Now the cry is for all things new. We cannot stand against change, and we do not try. We expect change even when we do not welcome it, since if we do not seek to control and curb it and indeed to master it, we will become puppets, corks swept along on its flood tide. I cannot, in fact, put it better than did Edward Heath, when he gave a lecture eighteen months ago in London paying tribute to the late Iain Macleod, a voice for which we are the poorer in Britain since it was stilled.

> Where once the binding cement of our society was a respect for authority at every level, we now have to trust in the influence of reason, the power of fair argument and the maintenance of values which we as Britons have inherited. That is now the fact—and anybody who acts in disregard of the requirements of fairness and reason, whether political party, trades union, employer, journalist or broadcaster, damages the only bond which today holds us together in society.

I started, you will notice, not with doctrine but with people, with individual men and women in their own lives. I believe that my society, and the type of democratic government which you share, have given people a better deal and a higher standard of life than ever before in our history. They are better housed, they are taught in finer schools, they have more cars, more radios, and television sets, more creature comforts than ever before. These are the achievements of the twentieth century. And in the seventy-five years of that story, in our collectivist age—in which in almost all countries the state plays a major role in life—Britain has been governed by the Conservative Party or by national governments of which it was the major part for not less than fifty years. Even at the last election the Labour government had only 38 percent of the votes cast, only 29 percent of the possible electorate. At least two out of three of all our people are in the center or on the right of the political spectrum. Indeed, as left-wingers in the present government, or as individual trade union leaders who are Communists seek to drive us in a leftward direction, perhaps we need some guarantees in our democracy to protect what are not just the rights of minorities but the rights of the majority itself, against the unrepresentative politics of willful, conspiratorial, and sometimes treasonable men.

You in this country a century ago had a large minority, the South, which needed protection against the majority. That minority went to war to fight for its rights. Just as the protection of a key minority group mattered constitutionally in the U. S. in the 1850s, so today it is not just individuals and minorities but majorities that need protecting against the tyranny of the state. In Britain in 1975, as in the U. S. in 1861, the "tyranny of the multitude," to adapt a phrase of Burke's, when controlled by willful men can be "a multiplied tyranny."

The rule of law is under threat in Britain. It is so in part because we have too many laws; seventy major Acts in this last session alone, now regularly at least fifty new Acts every session, all drafted hurriedly, full of errors and loopholes, and addenda, and sometimes hand-written amendments drawn up in the course of debates, not to mention quarterly budgets, with quarterly schedules and appendices, instead of annual finance bills. As a result we need more and more ombudsmen to investigate the injustices perpetrated by more and more draftsmen, serving the whims of more and more politicians.

We also have too many ministers with powers to make orders under Acts of Parliament, steadily, anonymously and bureaucratically restricting the range of individual freedom. The dangers are becoming even more sinister as instant government by White Paper has now been introduced, under both Conservative and Labour administrations. And these White Papers, now often prefaced by Green Papers, have led to Acts of Parliament with retrospective powers. Retrospective legislation is always destructive of the rule of law, and should have no place in Tory thinking.

There are again too many instances where the law has been brought into disrepute. May I illustrate the point by a quotation from Justice Donaldson's judgment in *Langstron* v *Amalgamated Union of Engineering Workers* and another, in the Industrial Relations Court on May 22, 1974.

The AUEW had adopted the policy with regard to the Act, such as had not been seen for centuries. It had denied Parliament's authority to legislate without first securing its approval. It had denied the authority of Industrial Tribunals and the court to administer the Act, even for the benefit of its own members. It had denied the democratic rights of the community to make laws which bound everyone. Above all, it was

blind to the wider consequences of such an unconstitutional
approach. If the Union could veto laws which did not appeal
to it, why should others not do the same? That way lay tyranny
or anarchy.

Indeed, May 1974 was a stormy month for democracy,
for at columns 228-343 in *Hansard* for May 7, 1974, may
be read an account of the Second Reading Debate on the
Trade Union and Labour Relations Bill, which contained
Michael Foot's reference to "some fool or some trigger-
happy judicial finger" (col. 239). So much for the independence of the judiciary and the attitude of some Labour
ministers. Ministers of the Crown hold office, are maintained in office, and rely for effective office, wholly upon
the rule of law. To undermine the authority of the law, or
the judges who administer it, is symptomatic of a serious
disease which should be fatal for a Minister of the Crown.
The political commitment of the left wing has even led to a
member of the cabinet exonerating the Clay Cross Coun-
cillors, who had broken a law passed by a previous government.

Examples abound of the erosion of rights previously
guaranteed by the law. Tories should examine carefully
every Parliamentary measure, even those brought forward
by a Conservative government. Consider the interference
with the sanctity of contracts resulting from legislation
freezing wages and rents. The Labour government permitted
tenants occupying the residue of long leases to acquire the
freeholds of their houses, thus denying the landlord's freehold title which he had previously supposed to be his by
right of law. The Labour government's Community Land
Bill indicates that the freehold will be compulsorily acquired,

merely upon the application for planning permission. None of these instances can be defended. Too many illegalities are condoned or backed by government itself.

But, there is another sense in which the rule of law is important to the individual. Not only must it regulate political democracy, but it must also provide for the maintenance of a stable society, and ensure law and order. Crimes involving violence are on the increase, with us as with you. Such crimes can be anything from violent picketing (assault and battery), through muggings, to murder. The individual citizen, generally speaking, wishes nothing better than to be left in peace to see his family prosper. To this end he is prepared to meet the cost of maintaining a police force, and to countenance the use of an army to separate belligerents in a civil war, as in Northern Ireland. The government's duty is to keep control of internal situations, in the interests of the law-abiding majority—in this regard they must, from time to time, be prepared to use that degree of force which the circumstances indicate is necessary. You have your problems of law and order in cities like New York, Detroit, and Dallas. We have ours in Ulster.

The essential authority implicit in the rule of law depends upon four ingredients:

1. That the government comprehend that law be accepted as just.
2. That the government introduce legislation on the basis of the "absolute supremacy ... of regular law, as opposed to the influence of arbitrary power." (Dicey)
3. That the government ensure and maintain that all are equal before the law, and that all are bound by it.

4. That the government allow changes in the law only through established democratic procedures, and not in response to unlawful pressures.

To a large extent these concepts are now under attack in Britain, and can only be reinforced by re-establishing the authority of government and the sovereignty of Parliament, and by maintaining the independence of the judiciary and its freedom from interference. Only under a Tory government will the rule of law be safeguarded.

I am not alone in voicing such fears. Lord Hailsham has been campaigning along these lines for six years. Four months ago he wrote in *The Times* that since the miners' strike of 1972:

There seems to me to be at least three major questions which may prove impossible to solve on the established assumptions of parliamentary supremacy.

The first of these is the inability of Parliament to cope with the ability of relatively small groups especially in the nationalised industries to extort virtually everything they wish to demand by bringing, or threatening to bring, the whole structure of civilized life to a standstill, either nationally or in a local community. To my mind this is by far the most potent factor in our current inflation.

The second of these is the failure of Parliament to meet the legitimate requirements for local democracy in Scotland and Wales and, it may be, in the English regions. So long as the business of government was as severely limited as it was before 1939, these feelings of local frustration, even when based on a regional nationalism, were dormant, indeed had no effective popular appeal. But the business of government is now all-embracing, and the power of the individual or the local community so small in relation to it, that separatist tendencies seem to me to command a support quite disproportionate to their real merits.

This brings me to the third, and it may be the most important, of the three questions, the inability of Parliament to respond to the need to protect the individual or minority or individual groups against decisions of the executive.

Given that these questions are unresolved and given economic conditions likely to create an almost revolutionary situation, it does not seem to me to be impossible any longer to disregard a constitutional change of a more comprehensive kind than has been seen since the Hanoverian succession. . . .

He advocates quite frankly a written constitution. Others, like Sir Keith Joseph, have called for a bill of rights.

For the central trend of our time is the growth of state power. Lord Chief Justice Hewart recognized it more than forty years ago when he called it *The New Despotism.* It was not new then, but it has grown by what it feeds on. Compulsory purchase orders and slum clearance orders have appropriated hundreds of thousands of homes, devalued them and held areas blighted and deserted for decades— often for arbitrary reasons and with little chance for owners or residents to object.

Some local authorities are convinced that they can emulate developers and make fortunes by large city-center developments and vastly expand their rate-base. So, they compulsorily acquire houses and shops, all of which have been servicing the public and providing their owners with a living earned usefully and in dignity. The compulsory purchase order rides in front of the borough bulldozer.

What overriding social and economic goal has been achieved by the compulsory purchase orders and slum clearance? It is now commonplace to say, though there were always those who said it, that it would have been far more economic to rehabilitate most—not all—of the hundreds of thousands of homes destroyed than to bulldoze them; it is now realized that bulldozing did great social harm, destroying communities as well as property, and that many council estates were bound to become focuses of social pathology. This, too, was known a long time ago, but it has not stopped the bulldozers churning.

The signs are everywhere. In the name of Parliament, and whether or not it represents the idea of law, the legislator intrudes into every aspect of life: abortion and divorce, homosexuality and drink. The general will has been replaced not by the will of all but by the will of a few who choose causes that will give them headlines. Tax policy is used to destroy small and independent businesses. The freedom of the press is threatened by the recommendation that only members of the journalist's trade union can write for the press, and by the sanction of other trade unions that particular leaders or advertisements shall not appear in print. And property in particular is under threat. Property to those who preach class war is always target number one. But property is the first of the genuine rights. Without property and individual economic rights all other rights are insecure. It was no accident that Jefferson's first draft of the Declaration of Independence spoke not of "life, liberty and the pursuit of happiness," but of "life, liberty and property." Once the state—which means politicians and bureaucrats—can take away your property, including your home and your income, restrict your right to earn your living, make you dependent on them for the kind of health service you receive, where and how your children will be educated, how and when you may travel abroad, your access to other freedoms will be in danger too. Freedom of speech means access to communications media; freedom of the press is possible only when people have the resources to start up publications and solicit support and subscriptions as best they can.

When the party-state controls jobs in management and the professions, when the unions and shop stewards control jobs at a manual level, it takes a bold man or a foolhardy one to speak his mind. Look at any socialist state. When governments have reduced private industry to near bankruptcy, so that without some sort of government aid they cannot continue, which industrialist will talk openly?

Respect for the law traditionally has been deep-rooted in Britain. It grew with the years, reflecting a belief in the rightness of the law, which had grown up slowly, and adapted slowly but surely to change. Things are quite different now, when highly political, controversial and far--reaching legislation abrogating traditional rights is churned out by Parliament casually, speedily, unceasingly. Governments who receive a minority of the poll and with it the support of an even smaller minority of all citizens, use the majesty of the law to dress up their prejudices and panic expedients. But this has inevitably undermined respect for the law in general. If some people or groups—be they trade unionists or ratepayers—can enjoy widespread sympathy when they defy politically unpopular laws, the next step is for people to defy any laws they find inconvenient.

Which brings me back to natural justice and the need to embody it in law. Until recently, people of all classes regarded the law as basically just. The Marxist minority would call it "class law," more out of habit than from immediate conviction, but the public was not with them. Today, the law is becoming a party-political football. If we are to save the law from Parliament, and Parliament from itself, we need a new safeguard.

I believe we need a bill of rights, and we have set up a committee to look into it. I believe it the more because the same forces are at work in local government, now large, unwieldy and bureaucratic machines.

Local authorities' activities, in particular, have grown in control over contracts for supplying goods and services, and for building works, over land use, and by participation in comprehensive developments. Use of joint purchasing powers by larger authorities and a public ownership of urban development land would increase the concentration of power in the public sector.

I am not alone in arguing this. Lord Scarman, in last year's Hamlyn Lectures, concludes from his appraisal of the conditions of laws and the citizen today, that a new settlement is needed to replace that of 1689, which gave Parliament unfettered sovereignty, which it did not press to excess for another two and a half centuries. He approaches the question from a different direction: much of what he writes could be called "progressive." But he reaches the same conclusion: to maintain a just society—he argues—we must preserve the rule of law. But the sovereign power of Parliament as wielded in our days, "more often than not exercised at the will of an executive sustained by an impregnable majority, has brought about the modern imbalance in the legal system. The common law is no longer the strong independent ally but the servant of Parliament. This perhaps did not matter quite so much as long as the constitution of Parliament itself contained effective restraints upon the will of a bare majority in one House. . . . The less internal control Parliament is prepared to accept, the greater the need for a constitutional settlement protecting entrenched provisions in the field of fundamental human rights, and the universality of the rule of law . . . ."

He therefore proposes "a new constitutional settlement replacing that of 1689 to be worked out by Parliament, the judges, the Law Commission and the government. . . . Its basis should be entrenched provisions (including a Bill of Rights) protecting it from attack by a bare majority in Parliament; a supreme court of the United Kingdom charged with the duty of protecting the Constitution."

As a first step to a written constitution, a bill of rights guaranteeing inter alia editorial freedom, the rights of union members and non-members, repealing the Official Secrets Act, guaranteeing the "right to privacy," the right to choice outside and inside the state system in health and education, the abolition of corporal punishment in schools, to be replaced by sanctions such as "exclusion," reduction of compulsory school-leaving age, etc.

I emphasize as central to my view of the free society the acceptance of the rule of law. I emphasize it because the New Leviathan, the state, is now matched in our society by a rival Leviathan, quite as unwieldy, almost as bureaucratic, constitutionally irresponsible, itself divided and at odds with itself, but now constituting a serious rival body to the State, the Trade Unions Congress. It is by no means inclusive of all workers, but it claims to speak for them. Of course it does not speak for the 7 million pensioners, or for the 13 million mothers, or obviously for 14.5 million children. In 1974 just over 10 million employees were members of unions affiliated to the TUC, out of a total work force of 24 million. Unlike the countries of the EEC, and especially unlike Western Germany with its 16 unions in the Deutcher Gewerkschaftsbund (DGB), Britain has no fewer than 495 unions, but many of them are small craft unions. Of the 110 unions in the TUC, unionization is almost total in coal, rail, steel and power supply, all in the public sector; it is high in heavy engineering and manufacturing. White collar unions like NALGO and ASTMS are growing steadily in numbers. Three quarters of Labour Party income comes from the unions, and they are certainly the party's major paymaster. Union income in 1973 was estimated at £70 million, and one union (TGNU) has over £20 million—invested, one notes, only to the extent of one-third of it in British equities. Unlike 1926, therefore, strikes in coal or public transport can bring whole industries and indeed the whole country to a halt, as in 1974, when the miners struck against a Conservative government's income policy and its fight against inflation.

The TUC is the economic wing of the Labour Party. Since the repeal of the Trades Disputes Act of 1927 the political funds of the unions have been the major source of Labour Party income, and the unions also control a number of parliamentary seats. The majority of trade unionists are moderate and patriotic men and women—one in three of whom in fact votes Tory. But they are led by the most militant, some of whom are avowed Communists. Most of the others do not support militants like McGahey, Scargill, or Scanlon. They know that strikes weaken companies, deter investment, lose exports and eventually jobs, and they are beginning to recognize that the rising tide of inflation is threatening the whole base of Britain's economy.

The Labour Party emerged in the first decade of the twentieth century as a group of trade union representatives in Parliament, and it has retained very close constitutional and financial links with the unions ever since. Twelve of the twenty-six members of the party's National Executive Committee are elected by the trade union delegates to the Party Conference, and in the ballots for the treasurer and five women members, trade union votes at the conference predominate. The union voting strength at the conference is normally about seven times that of the constituency delegates. Over 80 percent of members of unions with political funds pay a levy—in the case of three of the largest unions, between 30 pence and 40 pence a year per member—which goes to the Labour Party; in 1973 the unions paid a total of £670,000 out of a total Labour Party income of £870,000. Of the Labour M.P.'s elected in October 1974, 129 of 319 were sponsored and aided by the unions. The unions also help Labour through "education," propaganda, and organizational help at election times.

Yet in return trade unionists have derived little benefit from successive Labour governments. Unemployment rose when Labour was in office from 1964-1970, and this period also saw a statutory freeze in wages followed by a period of restraint.

Since the days of Disraeli, the Conservatives have favored

the rights of unions, within the law, to organize people at work. Liberal and Labour passed acts that virtually put the unions beyond the law; but for decades the Conservatives did not interfere with this position in the hope of preserving good industrial relations and obtaining reform by voluntary means.

By the late 60s, the position had so far deteriorated that even a Labour government attempting legislation (based on *In Place of Strife*) was to be frustrated by its left-wing and union-nominated M.P.'s. Harold Wilson said himself that "the Cabinet turned yellow." On gaining power in 1970, the Conservatives attempted to fill the vacuum along lines which all evidence suggests were then supported by a majority of the electorate.

This provided legal restraints on the exercise of the strike weapon in breach of contract; legal remedies for disputes and redress of complaints of unfair dismissal, both for the first time; and protection for individual union members and other employees. The code of Industrial Relations Practice and the provisions on unfair dismissal have been retained by the present Labour government which has swept away the rest of the Conservative 1971 legislation.

Moderate opinion across all three political parties regarded the act as performing a potentially valuable service to orderly industrial relations. In some fields, e. g., settlement of unfair dismissal disputes, it worked well. But overall it was distorted by some Labour politicians and union leaders, and was blamed for strikes which were in fact caused by pay claims.

The last Conservative government was the first to initiate wide-ranging talks over the whole field of economic and social policy with the representatives of British industry and the trade unions, in an effort to overcome the already dangerous inflationary crisis on an agreed basis. One of the subjects the government was prepared to discuss was the amendment of the Industrial Relations Act. Although a program of voluntary pay restraint could not be agreed, sufficient harmony was obtained to ensure the success of the Conservatives' pay policies during 1973, with days lost in strikes greatly reduced on previous years. This lasted until the whole policy was challenged by the National Union of Mineworkers in 1974.

No government measures can possibly succeed in halting the present wage-hyperinflation unless they effectively and radically reduce the collective bargaining power of the unions and their ability to enforce their will by strikes. Thus penal legislation is needed. It is not simply the physical question of getting down the percentage inflation rate, vital though that is. More important is the matter of morale. For all those who hold authority and make decisions in Britain—who have to meet union leaders in daily combat—it is essential for the government to demonstrate that the unions are not invincible, and above all that they are not above the law and constitution.

Already, trade unions appear to be exempt from an expanding range of laws and penalties. The number of instances in which unions censor newspapers is increasing. It is now very difficult for the police to secure the conviction of a trade union militant who breaks the law, or, if he is imprisoned, to keep him there. The law of picketing is brushed aside. Many people go around in fear of union "punishment," and the authorities are powerless to protect them. The issue of wage inflation, for which union action is now wholly responsible, is central to the management of the whole economy, and therefore must be the chosen battleground. But it is by no means the only issue. What those who make decisions, whether they be managers or civil servants, want to know, and know urgently, is whether authority ultimately lies with a democratically elected Parliament or with individual trade union leaders.

For this reason, it is not enough for our recurring crisis packages to be "acceptable" to the TUC, and evoke mutterings from merely the more incorrigible general secretaries. There has to be, and it has to be seen to be, a definite and unqualified defeat for trade union demands, a public and sharp reversal of the drift of recent years. The power of the trade unions has increased, is increasing, and ought to be diminished.

No country with a settled constitutional tradition, like Britain, has ever survived inflation at our present rate without a change of regime, usually achieved through violence. We are plainly heading straight in that direction. Nor is inflation the worst of the evils which spring from trade union omnipotence. The degree of overmanning which is now spreading through British manufacturing and service industries, and which is enforced by trade union actions and prohibitions, is unprecedented in any major industrial power.

Now I realize that I lay myself open to the charge of "union-bashing." But I restate my premise: Conservatives are keepers of the middle ground. In the Middle Ages we had to discipline the monarch—it took some seven centuries. In the nineteenth century we had to discipline some employers by factory legislation, some railway barons, and often some landowners. Each and all had to be brought into the framework of the law. Nowadays dukes sell their estates, often to nationalized industries, which being public have open-ended checkbooks, or set up zoos and teashops for tourists, including American. They have been curbed, first and last, by high taxes and death duties. You know the story: you had robber barons, too, even if to their achievements your own phenomenal economic advance was largely due. J. D. Rockefeller; Henry Ford; our own, and your, Andrew Carnegie, whose benevolence to his native Scotland, as well as to his adopted country, is literally incalculable; J. P. Morgan—all were men who never sat in Congress and yet thought of themselves as having it to command. You too had your senators for interests, for timber, oil, maize, and cattle. In the end, by one device or another you brought the special interests, the power and muscle men to heel, by the Interstate Commerce Commission, by "trust busting" and anti-monopoly legislation, by the vigilance of the courts, by having binding labor contracts durable for periods of years. We too curbed our overmighty subjects, coal owners by nationalization, landowners by death duties and land taxes, so that Britain and Sweden are the most heavily directly-taxed countries in human history. And it is right that all such special and privileged groups should be curbed. All of them. Today it is the trade union movement, itself incapable of governing itself, at the mercy of shop stewards, and led by men elected on tiny minority support in ill-attended meetings, that is the serious threat to our economy, our Parliamentary system, and society. It is the Overmighty Subject today.

I believe that our act in 1971 was on the right lines, just as indeed was Harold Wilson's abortive legislation of 1969. It limited lawful strikes and what the act defines as "irregular industrial action short of a strike" in two ways. First, it outlawed strikes or other such actions if they involved individuals breaching their employment contracts or are called by non-registered unions or by unauthorized representatives of registered unions. Second, the act listed about twenty-five "unfair" industrial practices by employers, unions and individuals, and lays down that unions should not discipline members who refuse to take part in them or in similar non-industrial action. There were also other measures designed to achieve the same end; all labor agreements were assumed to be binding, restrictions on sympathy strikers tightened, and "emergency" procedures laid down which the government could implement via the National Industrial Relations Court to stop industrial action against the public interest. I accept that the time may not be ripe for another major piece of legislation. But what are clearly necessary are some immediate plans.

1. We need to investigate the financial incentives and disincentives which are given to trade unions: at present strikers are entitled to repayments of income tax under Pay As You Earn and the family to supplementary benefits, which include the payment of rent, other outgoings that can be financed at the discretion of the Supplementary Benefits Commission, and a scale rate for a wife and children. Between 1951 and 1966 the cost of strikes to the Supplementary Benefits Commission was on average £1.2 million; in 1967 £490,000; in 1968 £414,000; and in 1969 £1.417 million; in 1970 £2.5 million, and in

1971 £4.4 million. The right to strike is basic to the British trade union movement, but it is a privilege whose cost should be borne by the strikers, not by the general public. If a striker's family is in serious need, supplementary benefit should be given it. But the present system whereby benefits are given on demand means in effect that society is subsidizing strikes. Once again, if there is an element of genuine cost-push inflation in the present inflation, the easy subsidies encourage rather than discourage strikes.

Pending more fundamental measures to curb the monopoly power of the trade unions—as real a threat today as monopoly power of landowners or coal owners ever was in the past—we should stop subsidizing strikes by making all security payments to strikers' families into loans recoverable through PAYE. Tax rebates to strikers should be given no more quickly than to other citizens.

2. We need a compulsory, secret, and postal ballot, independently counted and if necessary publicly financed. We need to ensure that unions can meet in company time, on company property, and with the consent and approval of the company, to ensure better attendance. I believe that the overwhelming majority of trade unionists would support such provisions.

3. I do not believe that we need a new law on picketing. What I do want to ensure is that the law on it is enforced: persuasion yes, violence and law-breaking never.

4. In the longer term we need to investigate and enforce no-strike contracts in vital industries like fuel and power. There seems to me an even more disturbing feature of

our age. Behind the denigration of authority, the growth of ever new Leviathans and the plethora of bureaucracies great and small—more than half the British working population is now engaged in government or in service industries and less than half in manufacturing and production—behind all this is a new justification for ever more ministers and ever more bureaucrats: the idea of social or redistributive justice. Our codes of action are no longer determined by what an individual chooses to do, but by the government's or society's view of what is just, determined by a few men acting in its name according to their view of fairness, rarely elected men, and even more rarely representative men. This social concern—genuine to some, a device to others—takes many forms. A few months ago the fashionable phrase was the social contract, by which it was claimed the trade unions had agreed to act cooperatively. Nowadays the talk is of the social wage. Like all the rest, it is a great nonsense, entirely ill-defined and unagreed, but legitimized by the word "social."

I cannot emphasize too strongly as a lawyer the importance of such words and of their precise meaning. I suggest to you—and you are well equipped to practice it—the old rule that when you don't know what a word means substitute "blah" for it. You will be surprised how many adjectives are surplus to requirement, and how much blah politicians talk. We have had a rich example of this recently in "The White Paper on Deflation." At one point the anti-inflation policy was the "law of the land," at another it was "a voluntary incomes policy." Which is it really? We have had also the sixteen page follow-up to it, sent by post to every home at a cost of £2 million, drafted by a man specially appointed, and paid a salary of £12,000 a year to do the job. It is not only the economy that is inflated, but words and their users—inflated and cheapened.

We expect tyrants to belong, in Lincoln's words, to "the family of the lion or the tribe of the eagle." But tyranny can spring from mediocrity, and despotism from inferiority, and be all the more dangerous for that. The ambition we should beware of—Michael Oakeshott warned us twenty years ago—is "the petty ambition to keep on the crest of the wave, the ambition which is satisfied with the illusion of affairs." In today's world of media images and instant impressions, and in which the truth quickly disappears behind foggy barrages of loaded words, freedom is easily lost, and our illusions prove to be costly and deadly. Tyranny doesn't need to be accompanied by a *coup d'etat*, or by a guillotine. In a little book on socialism written thirty years ago by John Parker, who is still an M.P., Parker estimated that by 1950 over six million people would be employed in what he called "public concerns." The figure is now twice that. He said that socialism would have arrived in Britain when "the majority of the working population are employed by public concerns of one sort or another." By that measure, it arrived a decade ago. It came insidiously, by way of bureaucracy and the endless battering of words and images. We are its prisoners. The time has come—to continue the Rousseauist metaphors—to break the chains.

Words, however, are the tools of all revolution, whether peaceful or violent: whether used by Danton or Robespierre, Lenin or Trotsky, Hitler or Mussolini—or Thomas Jefferson. "All men," he said, "are created equal." It was, he said, a self-evident truth. And he meant, it seems, political equality, not equality in the sight of God, but political equality even though at that time only a few landholders had the ballot, and slaves and those without property of course did not. A somewhat uncomfortable slave owner all his life, Jefferson never in fact proposed anything so radical as one man, one vote, and still less one man, one woman, one vote. But his eloquent phrase has survived in American politics as a challenge and an embarrassment, requiring a succession of subtle legal compromises, such as the separate-but-equal doctrine where education was concerned. With the nation's 200th birthday approaching, the courts at last have decided that legal equality in all its aspects means just what it says. With racially mixed juries, blacks now increasingly know full equality before the law.

The British attitude has been considerably different. "Equality before the law we all take as a matter of course," said Matthew Arnold, but when people talk of equality, he pointed out, "we understand social equality." The England of Arnold's nineteenth century, far more than the England of today, sang with enthusiasm the words of the hymn:

The rich man in his castle
The poor man at his gate,
God made them high or lowly,
And order'd their estate.

He regarded inequality as *the* religion of England.

That was never good American doctrine, which always despised frozen privileges, nobility, precedent, and rank. In America, so the theory went, anyone could better his lot, whatever the circumstances of his birth. Equality, in the sense of everyone's sharing alike, inspired a few utopians, but most Americans put their trust in equality of opportunity. In its name, education has been more lavishly endowed and widely dispensed than in any other nation in history. Of course, as the philosopher John Rawls notes, "Equality of opportunity means an equal chance to leave the less fortunate behind." The American, having improved his lot, says proudly, "I've *earned* what I've got."

And yet here again between the utopia and the reality, between the word and the fact, lies a vast gulf. Actually, the American way of life is characterized by a delicate interplay between inequality and equality. Inequality is the less talked about, but in fact the more fervently practiced. It is the great generator, inspiring the energy that spanned the American continent. It multiplies the wealth, sharpens the wits, creates the nervous dynamism that is called progress. The desire to excel is the adrenalin of competition. If winning does not matter, asked Adolph Rupp, former University of Kentucky basketball coach, why does anyone bother to keep score? I've always been struck by the fact in Britain that those who passionately advocate equality never apply it to football—they recognize inequality of talents there—or in athletics, in the theater, or the popstar world, in music, and in boxing. But, despite our real awareness of this, we have carried equality a long way in Britain. Our words may be spoken in a class accent, but I suspect that we are now much more egalitarian than you. Indeed a recent government report, the Diamond Report, proved it conclusively.

There is in both our countries an even greater danger. The talk is not just of social justice, the social contract, the social wage, but now of "social redress." As Rawls writes in *A Theory of Justice*, "Since the inequalities of birth and natural endowment are undeserved, these inequalities are to be somehow compensated for. In order to treat all persons equally, to provide genuine equality of opportunity, society must give more attention to those with fewer native assets and to those born into the less favorable social position."

And the Harvard sociologist Daniel Bell considers this "principle of redress," as Rawls calls it, to be "the central value problem" of contemporary society. How much redress? And at what cost to other groups in the society? Just how agonizing these questions can be is seen in the ongoing debate about busing and compensatory efforts. Where liberals like Bell once opposed discrimination because of "its denial of a justly earned place to a person on the basis of an unjust group attitude," now a different proposition is being argued. Merely being disadvantaged—by being black or female or young or Indian or whatever— *entitles* you to a favored place that is representative of the numbers in your category.

I am pleading for precision in speech and an end to this "social" mumbo-jumbo in order to reach precision of thought and analysis. For a politician it is a dangerous and divisive quicksand. I recall the story of the old lady who sought to flatter a speaker, could not find the right word, and said, "Your speech . . . it was absolutely . . . superfluous." Not to hurt her feelings but to show his sophistication lest he be overheard, he replied, "Thank you. I hope to publish it . . . posthumously." She replied, "Good! The sooner the better."

This is a harsh comment. It leads me to one—almost—final comment. Education is more rather than less essential in our would-be sophisticated society, swept by rumor, instant news and more instant comment. We need the best schools, and that means (a) that it is wrong to destroy, and deliberately destroy, existing good schools for the sake of a chimera, for schools are organic things, growing into their own special characteristics with the years, (b) variety of type, variety of approach, variety of institution. There is no one good school, whatever its label. There is a case for a comprehensive school where the resources are unlimited, where the school is custom-built, where the staff are dedicated and diverse. There is no case for deliberately interfering—by state decree—with local authority freedom or with parental choice, or with existing good schools. Moreover, the special quality of the British school system is its variety, with many independent schools, many direct grant schools, many parochial schools, for primarily Catholic churches, many non-fee-paying state schools. Socialism would reduce them all to a common and standardized school, of vast size, and go from a certainty on educational doctrine that all the evidence belies. It does not help the bright boy—who is due as much opportunity as the less gifted—to hold him back, nor help the less gifted to remind him constantly of his slower pace. We are all in fact, and in potential, profoundly unequal, and every child knows it. And I am for variety in schooling for the simple reason that the magic of good teaching defies analysis and all the pedagogical claptrap. At its best it might still just be Mark Hopkins at one end of the log and a keen child at the other.

In all the jargon of our age, some words have gone totally out of fashion. One of them is competition. It is by competition and rivalry that we all evolved—sad, but true. And the mark of true competition, I think, is its creativity, that it does break through thresholds. Of course there is bad and good competition, but I think, if I remove it, I put something much more insidious in its place: I put greed and envy and covetousness, which are precisely what our present society is riddled with. And I think if there is competition it has got to be tied to true reward, which is the second word in my vocabulary of recovery.

This is a plea for excellence, for variety, for the equal opportunities for unequal talents, for work and pride in it for its own sake, for creativity. It's a call for reality, and an end to utopias, and to the phony and the flatulent in politics. And central to all of it is the need for freedom. This freedom is the product of the exercise of the politician's function of preventing concentration of power and preventing uniformity of approach. Political freedom is inseparable from its own exercise, and from the diffusion of power. We all know Acton's phrase, "Absolute power corrupts absolutely." We forget that the next sentence read "All great men are bad." And economic freedom can spring only from the similar diffusion of economic power—and essentially of property ownership—as widely as possible.

I do not need to stress how essential to a free society is the fight against inflation. It destroys all confidence in a future to work for. It produces distortion of job description, and endless blackmail and barter. The weaker social groups are hardest hit, the old, the pensioner, the self-employed. Only the big battalions are safe. The injustice between one group and another, caused by the decline in the general value of money, produces immense social strains. The same process encourages the flight from savings into expenditure and from productive investment into land, Victorian chamber pots, and any assets which are believed to hold their value. It is crucial that savings be protected. It is imperative that investments if possible be encouraged. The succession of record profits, inevitably announced by companies during periods of heavy inflation, creates the impression among consumers and wage earners that the already rich and powerful are prospering at their expense, even though the reality is that much of industry is not generating enough surplus to cover replacement costs, and that dividends represent a rapidly decreasing share of national income.

Indeed, unless we end the threat of inflation our free political order is itself imperiled. It fell in Germany in the 1920s. It *can* happen in Britain too.

And freedom has to be defended, at home and abroad. We in our country—unlike you in yours—as I said at the outset, have been, unusually for us, free from war for a generation and from that national discipline that war compels. There have been minor wars in plenty, and they have been accompanied by new waves of terrorism and savagery: wars on the streets of Belfast and Londonderry; wars by bands in peaceable pubs and clubs and on street corners in London and Los Angeles, and across the world; wars in the name of national liberation or—again—of social justice, which usually have little to do with any real nation or with liberation, or with anybody's justice. Wherever the bomb is thrown or the dagger strikes, we are all the victims. All killing is murder, the more so when it is blind, indiscrimi-- nate, and cowardly. There are today as in the 1930s evil and violent men loose in the world. Against them every resource of the law must be invoked, and in such proven instances I believe that society should have the ultimate sanction of depriving them not only of liberty but of life. The enemy within is often part of the conspiracy of the enemy without. In the end we must fight for freedom.

Our democratic heritage is not frail but it is fragile. It could be destroyed by nuclear war from without and by sectional and personal egoism from within, by ideological intolerance, and by the creed of greed. To preserve it, and to use it as the springboard to peaceful advance calls for careful nurture, for zealous affection. Your own President F. D. Roosevelt spoke of being the good neighbor. I want us to be good neighbors on a common ocean, together guarding and extending our joint faith and common ground of freedom and of variety in the pursuit of excellence.

M. Stanton Evans

The Liberal Twilight

I have been on the Hillsdale campus on a number of occasions and always welcome the opportunity to return to an institution which is a bastion for traditional American ideals, the principles of the free enterprise system, and the basic affirmations of our constitutional Republic. I've known many of your faculty and staff people for a number of years, and am privileged to count Dr. Roche among my personal friends.

I was quite gratified by the flight here and this very nice weather. I fly a good deal commercially and I'm what is known in the trade as a white knuckle flyer, which means basically that I'm a coward. I have devoted considerable time to studying the aerodynamic characteristics of airplanes, and have concluded from that study that they are capable of falling down. As a result of that, whenever I fly, I always grip the seat rest very tightly and lift to give the elements a little help, and that tends to make the knuckles very rigid and white and prematurely arthritic.

I have not always had the kind of pleasant flight I had today and I have a little anecdote about one flight which I think is illustrative of some of the imponderable issues of our time. I was flying about six or eight months ago from what was then my home city of Indianapolis to New York. It was a very bad day. There was a lot of turbulence, a good deal of fog on the East Coast and electrical disturbance in the atmosphere. We had been tossing around for a good hour and a half or two hours, and I was getting very worried as I watched the lightning flash past the window.

At this point the pilot came on the squawk box. If you have flown much commercially lately, you are perhaps aware that pilots nowadays are not content simply to drive the airplane. They have become tour guides and masters of ceremonies. This pilot obviously had been watching the now defunct television show, "Laugh In," which was very popular a few years ago, since he came on with this rather frostbitten routine about the good news and the bad news.

He came on and said, "Good afternoon, I'm your pilot, Captain So and So. I have some good news and some bad news. I'll give you the bad news first, which is in essence that we are lost. Because of the fog on the East Coast we cannot get into New York—in fact we cannot see New York. We cannot proceed by visual flying rules. Because of the electrical disturbance in the atmosphere, most of our instruments are on the fritz. The radar is not transmitting information about other aircraft in the vicinity and the altimeter is not working, so we don't know how high we are. We have lost radio contact with the ground and beyond that, and even more serious, the electricity has caused the compass to gyrate wildly, so we don't really know in

what direction we are flying. That is the bad news. The
good news is that we have a 100 mile an hour tail wind
and we're an hour ahead of schedule."

I hasten to say that is a fictionalized version of our trip
to New York, but I think it is illustrative of a principle
which is frequently forgotten in our political discussions. It
illustrates the fact that a frequently used term in our
political discourse, the term "progress," is not a substantive
in and of itself. It is a term of relation, applicable only if
you know where you are and where you want to be. Only
if you have your proper compass bearings can you describe
a particular course of action as progress or the reverse. If
you do not have such compass bearings, then simply increasing the velocity at which you're traveling may be the
opposite of progress. It might take you farther and farther
away from where you want to be.

It is my contention that that is exactly the condition of
American public policy in this latter part of the twentieth
century. We are being told, to the point of monotony, that
if we want progress we must continue doing certain things
which are advocated in Washington, D. C. These things
consist essentially of reposing more and more power in the
hands of the federal government, creating new agencies to
monitor various aspects of our economic, political and
social life, imposing new taxes and extending new subsidies
to various components of our society—in general increasing
the scope and velocity of activities we have been pursuing
for the past four decades.

We can discover that this course of action is the opposite
of progress if we go back to the original compass bearings
which were set out for us by the people who created this

country. We have many difficulties in our society, but in one respect we're very fortunate. And that is the fact that there is nothing esoteric about the purposes of this American Republic of ours. Anyone who is reasonably literate and who has access to a public library or a college library, or indeed a private library of even modest dimensions, can go to the relevant documents and discover exactly what the American Republic was supposed to be all about.

If we perform that exercise, if we take a look at the Declaration of Independence and the Constitution, the debates in the federal convention in which the Constitution was hammered out, or in the state conventions in which it was ratified, or the *Federalist Papers,* or the writings of the great constitutional theoreticians of that formative era, such as John Adams and James Madison, we discover over and over again certain seminal ideas expressed with great clarity and at great length.

Their principal affirmations were as follows: first, that in all of our political arrangements, our foremost objective ought to be to extend as widely as possible the range of decision open to the individual, to enlarge the ambit of personal choice and to minimize the number of decisions that are made through the instruments of coercion. In short, a commitment to the primacy of human freedom, to the protection of the autonomy and integrity of the human person.

That is, in our contemporary debate as well as in historical debate, a pretty unexceptionable sentiment. If you ask most people if they believed in what I just said, I think they would say yes, why not? They believe in human freedom. But there is a second point, a second affirmation which makes the point a little more sharply. That was the founders' belief that, if you're going to get this enlargement of the range of individual decision, then you're going to have to do one thing above all others, and that is to limit the reach of governmental power. While they understood that government is a necessary institution in society, because it maintains that arena of order within which alone freedom can flourish, they understood as well that it is a dangerous institution because it is, in the final analysis, coercion. It is a legalized monopoly at force.

And if one person or one group of people can get that power into his hands or their hands, then he or they can ride roughshod over the liberties of everybody else. The government can then become a hazard to the very freedoms it was instituted to protect.

So our founders, emphasizing those two points, came up with a particular kind of government, which I call government by self-denying ordinance—known in the Anglo-American tradition as constitutional government: a government which is limited in and by the very settlement that creates it; which, even as it exists to constrain the actions of people in the society, is itself constrained by a prior understanding, a written document of some kind, which defines the scope of its powers. That was precisely the kind of government that our founders wanted.

They added to this a number of subsidiary constraints: specifically the doctrine of "enumerated powers" or states' rights, which said that the central government was given powers a, b, and c, and that all powers not so granted by the contracting agencies, the states, were reserved to the states respectively, or to the people. This is the language of the 10th Amendment, insisted upon by a majority of the states ratifying the Constitution. Their powers, as Madison put it, were "numerous and indefinite" as opposed to those of the central government, which were "few and defined." The founders added to that the classical notion of a counterpoise within the supreme authority, among the legislative, executive and the judicial branches, so that each would constrain the others and if one of them got out of line, the others would have the means and motive for doing something about it. And even that, they thought, was insufficient to safeguard freedom from the encroachments of government, so they added an explicit Bill of Rights.

So you have these four kinds of safeguards built into our system: the written Constitution, the doctrine of enumerated powers, the doctrine of divided powers, and, finally, the Bill of Rights itself, complexities and balances and checks and counterpoises throughout the design of the American Republic. I don't recite that to tell you something in general you already know, but to stress a point. And that is that the major preoccupation of the people who created the United States of America was precisely *to prevent the excessive concentration of political and economic power*. This was their overriding objective in doing all of these things, reflected over and over and over again in all of the constitutive documents of the founding era. Those are our compass bearings—the guidelines that tell us the objectives that this Republic is supposed to achieve and the governmental arrangements that are supposed to achieve them.

Now, if we take those compass bearings and compare them to what is happening in the United States today, and what has been happening for the past four decades, I think it is rather apparent that these fundamental emphases have been almost totally reversed. What we see occurring today is, in essence, the mirror image of the traditional imperatives. In place of the notion that it is preferable to have a system of voluntary exchange, we have the notion that people are too dumb to look out for themselves. If we leave them to their own devices they will make the wrong decisions, buy the wrong products, and exploit each other in the marketplace, they will pay insufficient wages or charge prices that are too high, or in general do things they ought not to do.

So, in the prevailing view, there needs to be some superintending intelligence above the people which prevents them from making wrong decisions. That superintending intelligence is, of course, the cadre of experts and engineers and members of the intellectual elite who have perceived the problem of popular stupidity, and who will make their judgment supreme over that of the people. They will plan things that people fail to plan for themselves.

That is a reversal of the first commitment of our political system. And having reversed that commitment, the planning mentality has necessarily reversed the second as well. If you're going to substitute expert judgment for lay judgment as rendered by the individual in the marketplace, you're going to need some kind of machinery to make that judgment stick. You're going to need some place to mobilize resources and allocate energies and push wages up and prices down, and to decide what's going to be produced and what isn't. You're going to need a mechanism for making all this happen. And that mechanism is the government.

As this notion has expanded in our society, we have seen a dramatic growth in the scope of government power: a drainage of power upward out of the states into the central government, and, within that central government, away from the Congress into the hands of the executive. And, I hasten to stress, not necessarily into the hands of the president, but into the hands of the executive bureaucracy.

As a result, we have established on the banks of the Potomac precisely the kind of unchecked, untethered monolithic power structure that our founding fathers wanted to avoid. This has been done on the basis of a number of arguments and alibis that need examination. One of these is the suggestion that the scope of federal power is not much larger than that which existed forty years ago. As a result of this activity, supposedly, we increase the absolute size of government, but since we are also increasing the productivity of our economy, relatively speaking there isn't that big an increase.

There are lots of ways of looking at that argument, but I think the simplest is to take the spending figures, and trace them down through this period of four or four and a half decades. If you go back to calendar year 1929, you discover that in that year, the entire outlay of the federal government came to less than $3 billion, $2.6 billion to be exact. If you come forward to fiscal '75, you discover that the outlay of the federal government was about $324 or $326 billion. If you round that back down just to $300 billion, you discover that in a span of 46 years, the budget outlays of the federal government increased by 10,000 percent, from 3 billion to 300 billion.

This was a period when the population of the United

States was increasing from about 120 million people to perhaps 214 million, an increase of roughly 75 percent. So in those terms it is readily apparent that the compulsory sector of our economy, just measuring the federal component of it, has been increasing at a rate much greater than the growth of the economy as a whole.

Now it is true that the increase in spending is measured in dollars devalued by the process of inflation. But it is possible to correct for that and to take the percentage of government spending in terms of gross national product or personal income, and thus to get a constant measure of what is happening to our economy. If we do that, we discover that in 1929 the percent of gross national product consumed by government at all levels was just about 10 percent. Today, it is 37 percent.

A single proposal now before Congress, the National Health Insurance Plan of Senator Kennedy, would increase that percentage to 45 percent. If the trend of growth that has prevailed for the past two decades continues simply as it has been with no major additions, by the year 2000 the percent of GNP absorbed by government is going to be 67 percent, according to the estimates of the Office of Management and Budget. In terms of personal income, the story is much the same. In 1930, the percent of personal income consumed by governments at all levels was 15 percent. Today it is 44 percent.

And that, I might stress, is only a threshold measurement. On top of the spending measures, you have layer upon layer of regulatory intervention which itself imposes social costs and economic costs not included in the budget figures. We know, for example, that there are, at various levels of government, 283 different agencies which have some species of superintendence over the activities of American business. We know that there are about 150,000 government employees at every level involved in that activity. We know that in the federal government alone there are 63,000 employees involved in such activity.

We know that in paperwork alone, the costs to business and taxpayers amount to about $40 billion a year, according to the studies of the Commission on Federal Paperwork, chaired by Representative Frank Horton of New York. We know that there are something like 6,000 different federal forms which have to be filled out by American businesses. President Ford's Council of Economic Advisors has estimated that the additional costs to consumers of various federal regulatory programs is $130 billion a year.

If we compare this level of intervention with the level prevailing in the explicitly collectivist countries, we find there is not much difference. The percent of GNP taken in the Scandinavian countries for social programs is not much higher than the percent which is being taken here. So the assurance that it's all in your mind, it's all relative and isn't really that big, is mistaken. But if that empirical point can be established, one finds other assurances and explanations forthcoming.

One of these is that the burden of guilt for all this spending rests on the military. We experience high taxes and ravaging inflation, allegedly, because we're spending so much money on unneeded military implements and responding to the pressures of the military-industrial complex.

That notion has been sold very effectively in many segments of the national media and by very articulate politicians. But it is totally unsupportable on the empirical record. If you examine the budget figures for the last decade, you discover that the percentage of the federal budget devoted to the military has been falling like a stone. In 1963, 46.9 percent of the federal budget went for defense, almost half. For fiscal '76, it's 27 percent, just a little over a quarter. Even though there has been an absolute dollar increase in outlays for defense, that proportion has fallen steadily because the major spending increases have been for non-defense items, and mostly for welfare.

It's interesting to note the spending history of the Department of Defense as put up against the spending history of the Department of Health, Education, and Welfare. In the two decades, 1952 to 1972, the DOD budget increased by 74 percent, which in constant dollars was not much of an increase at all. In fact, according to the Brookings Institution, that was roughly keeping even in terms of what could be purchased with the dollars.

In that same two decades when Pentagon spending increased by 74 percent, the spending of the Department of HEW increased 4,837 percent, from $1.9 billion to roughly $100 billion. Today, whatever one may think about the Department of Defense, it no longer has a distinction it once did have. That is, it is no longer the largest department of the federal government. Its budget for '76 is about $93 billion. The budget of the Department of HEW is $118 billion. That is where the truly enormous spending increases have occurred—not for defense but for domestic social welfare programs.

If that empirical point can be driven home, one encounters another explanation which also has its plausible aspects.

This is the suggestion that, even though we are spending all this money on social welfare programs, at least we are helping poor people. We are taking resources from people who don't need them and putting them into the hands of people who do. This is what all the transfer payment programs are about and they have indeed been growing very rapidly.

There is no question that some proportion of this enormous increase in federal spending has gone to help people who are in need. But I would suggest to you that is not the major impact of what has happened. The major impact is something else altogether.

Again we face the difficulty of how you quantify these things. I have a formula which I think suggests a kind of answer. It is possible to measure the net increase in social welfare spending over a given span of time. If we do that, we discover that between 1960 and 1971, the total level of expenditure on social welfare programs, broadly defined, increased from $50 billion in 1960 to $171 billion in 1971— about a $120 billion increase.

It so happens that, according to the Bureau of the Census, there are about 25 million poor people in the United States, defined as people with an income level of $4,137 or less for a given year, for a family of four. If we take those 25 million poor people and divide them into the $120 billion increase—*not* the whole thing, just the increase—we discover that if we had simply taken that money and given it to the poor people, we could have given each and every one of them an annual stipend of $4,800 a year, which means an income for a family of four of $19,200. That is, we could have made every poor person in America a relatively rich person. But we didn't. Those poor people are still out there.

What happened to the money? The answer is that some of it did get into hands of the people who are supposed to get it. But a lot of it didn't. I would say the majority of it went to people who are counseling the poor people, working on their problems, examining the difficulties of the inner city, trying to rescue poor families and devise strategies for getting them out of their doldrums. It went to social workers and counselors and planners and social engineers and urban renewal experts, and the assistant administrators to the administrative assistants who work for the federal government.

Now it is very interesting to note, if we talk about relative impoverishment and affluence in our society, that the level of income among people who work for the federal government is considerably *higher* than the level of income of people who work for private industry. In 1972 the median income for someone working for the federal government in civilian employment was about $12,700. The corresponding income for someone working in private industry was about $9,000. This means that whenever these programs are adopted, the gross effect—and I use the word in both its senses—is to transfer money from people who are relatively poor, that is, taxpayers, to people who are relatively well off, that is, people who work for the federal government.

It's also interesting to note the two most affluent counties in the United States. What do you think they are? Westchester County, New York? Dupage County, Illinois? Marin County, California? Orange County, California? No, none of those.

The two richest counties in the United States, according to median family income, are Montgomery County, Maryland, and Fairfax County, Virginia, which happen to be the two bedroom counties for the federal government. That's where the government workers live. The median family income in Montgomery in 1972 was $16,000 plus. In Fairfax, which was not quite so good, it was about $15,700. Every time a program is adopted to enhance the power of the federal government, to cure impoverishment, those are the people who are enriched.

So it seems to me that argument is implausible, although superficially appealing. We simply have not been assuaging poverty by what we're doing. The other justifications are essentially subdivisions of that one. They are contentions that in problem areas throughout our economy, it is necessary to have a federal intervention of some type because the private market economy and the system of voluntary exchange have failed to get the job done.

We need a new health care program, supposedly, because the system of private health care delivery has failed. We need a new spending program to create jobs because the private market economy has failed to provide jobs. We need a new housing program because the private housing construction industry fails to provide new low-income housing. We need environmental constraints, we need energy programs—all allegedly because the system of private exchange doesn't do the job.

It is precisely here, however, that the liberal social philosophy has reached a watershed which even liberal theoreticians have come to recognize as such. If one takes the read-outs on all these various programs and all of the difficulties that we are allegedly going to redress by enacting them, two things become apparent.

One is the fact that quite clearly these programs do not solve social problems. They are much more likely to *create* such problems. Second is the fact that in each and every one of these issue categories, you discover that every problem brought forward as a reason for further governmental intervention is the result of a *prior* intervention. The issue categories in which this is so are worth examining in a bit of detail because they show the phenomenon of self-generating interventions very clearly.

Inflation: We are being told that we have to have various kinds of government action because of rising oil prices or rising food prices. We've seen the enactment of a very complicated system of wage and price controls which obviously failed. We still have price controls in the energy field. We have exhortations on occasion to return to the system of full controls, all of this to cure the problem of inflation.

Well, who creates the problem of inflation? The answer is very plain on the record. Inflation, as I am sure the students of economics here are well aware, is essentially a phenomenon of more dollars chasing fewer goods, or an increasing money supply going after a relatively stable volume of production. That is exactly what has been happening in the United States in recent years. Take a look at what happened to the money supply between '67 and '73, right through the period of controls. In that span, the money supply increased by 44 percent. The index of industrial production increased only 26 percent. What happened to consumer prices? They were right in between the increase in industrial production and the increase in the money supply, rising by roughly 35 percent. It is very clear on that record, as well as on the theoretical articulation of what causes inflation, that government itself creates the problem government is setting out to cure.

Unemployment: Government wants to cure unemployment through spending programs and job training projects. This is indeed a serious problem. Adolescent unemployment is very high these days; specifically, unemployment among black adolescents has soared to about 40 percent, and one of the measures about a year ago was 41 percent. Now why is black adolescent unemployment that high? What has caused this very serious problem?

The cause of that phenomenon, as it happens, is a "humanitarian" social program called the statutory minimum wage, one of those ideas that sounds great in theory but is not so great in practice. The theory is that we can raise peoples' wages by *fiat*. We simply pass a law saying workers ought to be paid a living wage and it is inhuman to pay less than that wage and we will make it illegal to go below it.

Unfortunately, it doesn't work that way, because in the final analysis, everybody's wage is paid by the consumer. If a given employee doesn't bring to the job the skills and the education to generate what he or she is being paid, that employee isn't going to get hired, or will be the first to be laid off when the economic crunch arrives. This means that any statutory floor under wages always works to the disadvantage of marginal workers, the people who can least afford further disadvantage because they've already had insufficient education and training.

We see that in our economy precisely in the phenomenon of black adolescent unemployment. In 1954, the federal minimum wage stood at 75¢ an hour. Black adolescent unemployment was 16.5 percent, which was bad enough in itself. By 1968, however, the federal minimum had gone to $1.60 an hour and black adolescent unemployment was 26.5 percent. Now the minimum is $2.10 and it's going to go to $2.20, and black adolescent unemployment is 40 percent. So in this instance as well the federal government is creating the very problem it allegedly is setting about to cure. The answer to that problem is not further intervention into the market, but to phase out the intervention that we have.

Housing: We're told the private housing construction industry has failed. The record is directly the opposite. In the period since the 1930s, in which the federal government has been involved in housing programs of one sort or another, what has been the result of those programs? There have been many computations made and they all point to the same conclusion. The net impact of federal involvement in the field of housing has been the destruction of over one million units of housing. Now some of that housing, agreed, was unliveable, but much of it was liveable, and much of it was destroyed by urban renewal programs which went in to inner cities, obedient to the vision of the planners, and knocked down row after row, unit after unit of liveable housing and threw the tenants or the owners of that housing out and packed them into very densely populated neighborhoods elsewhere. Again, ironically enough, the principal victims of this program were black people, the very people who were supposed to be the major beneficiaries.

Now while the federal government was creating a net destruction of one million housing units, what was the private construction industry doing? The answer is that it was upgrading American housing in a chronicle of progress, true progress, that is probably unequalled anywhere in the annals of productive enterprise. In 1940, 51 percent of the housing in the United States was rated standard—that is, not in need of major repair, not overcrowded, with indoor plumbing. In the census of 1970 the corresponding figure was over 90 percent.

In the two decades, 1950 to 1970, private industry built over 30 million units of housing, more than doubling the supply of standard housing. So on the one hand, you have a record of continued and very impressive progress on the part of private business, on the other hand a record of destruction by the federal government, exactly the reverse of what is suggested in the liberal scenario.

The same kind of thing is true in the realm of transit, environmental controls, energy, and almost every other issue that is being debated in Washington. The liberal argument has the situation backwards. It is not government that can cure the problems generated by private enterprise, but private enterprise that alleviates and diminishes problems created by government.

There is finally, and perhaps most important of all, another assurance whose failure, in my opinion, indicates that we are entering a period of liberal twilight—a period in which the liberal world view as we have known it begins to fade from vision.

The final assurance is not economic but political and constitutional: that it is possible, on the one hand, to pile up all

these powers in the hands of the federal government, erod-
ing the barriers to the exercise of power built into the
constitutional system by our founding fathers, and yet
maintain our essential freedoms.

What's important, in the liberal view, are human rights or
rights of speech and advocacy and political association and
religion. These are the core values of a free society, and we
guarantee that even though we are doing all of these things
to the economy and to the constitutional system, that all
these rights are going to survive.

I regret to say that this final assurance is also unjustified,
according to an enormous body of evidence that is piling
up before us.

To begin with, it is theoretically impossible to reconcile
these propositions. If in fact one can control the *economic*
elements of a society, then one can control political activity as well. To take a very simple example, if one can
control the supply of newsprint, one can control the press.
It is interesting to recall that the closest we ever came to
seeing a mass shutdown of newspapers in this country was
in the fall and winter of 1973 when there were labor
problems in Canada and the supply of newsprint was diminished. The result was that newspapers all over the Midwest
cut back on the number of pages they could print, and
there was a very real fear that they would have to stop
publishing altogether. As a result of that particular economic constraint, a number of features and opinion columns
were dropped from newspapers—a very clear example of
economic factors impinging upon freedom of expression.

But there are other more direct illustrations as well. We
know, for example, that there is not freedom of political

communication today in a very large segment of the press, namely the electronic media. In that business the basic economic resource, the broadcast frequency, is controlled by the federal government—by the Federal Communications Commission. If you want to operate a commercial broadcasting station, you have to get a license from the FCC and that license is subject to renewal every three years.

If you do not conduct yourself in a manner the FCC considers appropriate, your license can be taken away. There are few instances in which licenses are actually removed but it isn't necessary to have many removed for the point to get across: if you conduct yourself peaceably and don't stir up lot of fuss and feathers, you probably will get a routine renewal. But if you create problems and become excessively controversial, as has happened in certain cases, then your license can be taken away. Hundreds of thousands, perhaps millions of dollars of revenue, can be lost as a result of that political decision.

Above and beyond this threshold constraint, the Federal Communications Commission has added other very explicit constraints through the fairness and equal time doctrines. The Federal Trade Commission has also gotten into the act with its rulings about commercial content. So the range of debate in commercial broadcasting has been severely constricted, principally because the basic economic resource is in the hands of the government.

During the Watergate controversy, there was a considerable flap when Senator Lowell Weicker of Connecticut, a maverick Republican on the Watergate Committee, came up with a document which allegedly had been drafted by Jeb Stuart Magruder, a functionary with the Committee to Re-elect the President.

In this memorandum, Magruder spelled out a number of ideas for getting at people in the media who disagreed with the administration. He said things like this: The first thing we do when we get Dean Burch appointed chairman of the FCC is to start monitoring what the networks are doing, and build a case that they are not providing balanced programming.

Then we can get Antitrust Division of the Justice Department to take a look at the networks and suggest that there are going to be actions on that score. And then we can get the IRS into the act and start taking a look at the tax situation. There are all kinds of things we can do to intimidate them and back them off a little.

When that came out it caused a tremendous uproar; there was indignation that the Nixon regime was planning to use the powers of government to punish dissenters. It reminded me of a very similar memorandum written back in the early 1960s by a man named Victor Reuther, one of the high officials of the United Auto Workers, addressed to then Attorney General Robert Kennedy. In that memorandum, Victor Reuther spelled out a scenario very similar to that spelled out by Magruder.

Reuther said, in essence, we should take the FCC and the IRS and other agencies of the government and start putting heat on conservative broadcasters creating problems for the Kennedy administration. He very elaborately suggested some of the things that might be done. That advice was acted upon. We know now that his program for inhibiting dissent through the political use of the Federal Communications Commission was pursued very energetically by both the Kennedy and Johnson administrations.

I cite those parallel examples not to say that since it was done under the Kennedy administration and the Johnson administration, therefore it's all right under the Nixon administration—no. Both are wrong. The point is otherwise. That point, it seems to me, is that in neither of these memoranda was it suggested that we needed a single *new* governmental power to control the media in this country. What was being suggested was that *the power is already here*. We *have* the power. Just take it and use it against the people who disagree with us.

Ultimately the Nixon attempt failed because of Watergate. But nonetheless, the power *was* there and the power is still there. That power has not been dismantled as a result of Watergate. It's all sitting there in Washington, D. C., waiting to be used by somebody who knows how to deploy it in sophisticated fashion.

A second point implicit in what I've been saying is that almost all of these controls are economic in nature. All have to do with controlling some aspect of our economic lives, either through taxation, antitrust, or the FCC licensing power. By controlling the economy, we control political expression as well.

Alexander Hamilton said a power over a man's subsistence amounts to a power over his will. A very true and very obvious statement. If I could control the wherewithal of your life, I could control almost everything about you. If I can control your subsistence and I can control your will, I can certainly control your voice or pen.

In essence what the liberals have attempted to do, and it has been a heroic enterprise in its way, has been to abandon the premises of a free society, to adopt the premises of an authoritarian society, and yet to avoid the authoritarian result: to say that we're going to have a collectivized, regimented society and still maintain our libertarian values. What is happening to us now, in the terminal phase of that experiment, is a final disintegration of libertarian values. We are beginning to see the indications of an authoritarian state—not simply a regimented state, but an explicitly authoritarian state—crop up around us.

I think we see this in some very mundane, very ordinary controversies debated all the time in communities around this country. The issues I pick are essentially three—busing, sex education, and the population issue.

Take a look at those issues. The usual debate on busing, for example, is as follows. The proponents of the neighborhood school who want to preserve their local neighborhood and autonomy against the people who want to get authentically integrated schools, and all the debate is about "unitary" and "dual" systems and *de jure* and *de facto* segregation.

But if one pursues the busing controversy to its heart, one discovers a totally different set of issues. If you go back and read the Coleman Report, published in 1966 by the Department of Health, Education and Welfare—named for Professor James Coleman, then of Johns Hopkins, now of Chicago—you find the rationale for busing spelled out pretty plainly. And it is articulated even further in another document called *Racial Isolation in the Public Schools,* published in 1967.

The Coleman Report in essence was a review of all the factors entering into public education and the things that resulted from those factors. It found that the enormous increase in spending for public schools over the past several decades had not resulted in a corresponding increase in learning gains, and in particular had not produced any diminution in the black-white learning gap which was observed at the beginning of school and was still observed at the end of school.

The problem as it was perceived by these researchers, and those explaining their research, was that we were sending black kids into these wonderfully appointed, very expensive public schools with all the right facilities and all the right preparation, and there we were programming into them the good things they ought to know. But then at the end of their school they were going home to their ignorant parents, where the good effects of the offical programming were being washed away. They were slipping back into the same culture pattern from which they had originally emerged.

The conclusion drawn from that—to put it in its most brutal but I think most accurate form—was that we *had* to *break the link between the black child and his or her parents*. We had to take that child and get him away from the influence of his parents and immerse him as fully as possible in an artificial environment created by planners who had the proper credentials and the proper expertise and the backing of the state.

Coleman said it very plainly in an article in *The Public Interest* in the summer of 1966. He said that what is needed is a school that begins very early in the day and ends very late in the day, a school that preferably would begin very early in life. We had to replace the home environment by an artificial environment.

Now that's a very interesting idea, and it is particularly

interesting when it is proposed in the name of civil rights—
to take the black child as an experimental guinea pig in
cultural homogenization, and to say that we're going to get
that child away from his family and to mold him according
to a design concocted by official planners.

It is this same idea that is apparent beneath the surface
in these other controversies. We see it in the sex education
debate—and again the superficial level is one thing and the
actual level is something else. The superficial, public level
is: My kid is being exposed to pornography because they
are showing him pictures of frogs copulating. On the other
side is the school saying the kids have to learn hygiene and
how to avoid getting pregnant, and it's important that we
teach them these things.

Again, I'm not downplaying the importance of such
issues, but they're not the real issues. The real issues are
essentially the same as in the busing controversy. If you
push that one far enough, you invariably reach a point
where people on the side of the sex education programs
say: Look. Let's face it. These parents are too dumb.
They don't know what is right for their own kids. They've
got all these hang-ups and can't talk to the kids about this.
They don't know how to shape them emotionally and
physically. We know. We've got the credentials. We studied
this. We've got the degrees and we've got the state backing
us up.

The population question is the ultimate version of this
whole controversy. A plausible rhetoric about the "quality
of life" would have us suppose that the issue here is
numbers of people. And, without taking a particular side,
that is an issue worth discussing. But it isn't the real issue.

The real issue isn't the *number* of people. It's the *kind* of people. Read the literature that has emerged from the abortion and euthanasia movements and examine the meaning of the phrase "quality of life." Sounds good, doesn't it? Everyone wants a better quality of life. Well what that means is something rather different. *It means that some lives are better than others*, that there is such a thing as a life that isn't worth living and that it is up to those of us who have the expertise to make the decision as to which lives are worth living and which aren't. And that is the payoff. That is the ultimate phase of this development in which the liberal mind set becomes transformed into something quite the opposite of liberal: in which the libertarian remnants that have persisted through these forty years fall away, and we see the emergence of an authoritarian state.

There is a well-known writer named Gore Vidal who has synthesized these notions very lucidly in the scholarly journal, *Playboy* magazine. In an interview, Mr. Vidal laid it right on the line—and he is, in most of his attitudes, a pluperfect liberal, I might add. He said what we need in this country is "an authority with the capital A," which would make the ultimate decisions about disposition of energies and resources in our society. I mean specifically by that the question of births, he said. Let's face it, some people simply aren't equipped to be parents. And those who aren't equipped should be prevented from having children. After all, he said, this is the way we raise animals, why not people?

I can point you to the exact page in *Mein Kampf* where the identical argument is rehearsed—in which it is stated that, after all, some people are not fit to procreate. Some people are not fit to be parents and they should not visit their unfitness on succeeding generations. A whole argument is developed on that score and the identical clincher is applied: After all, this is the way we raise animals. Why not people?

If one adopts the authoritarian premises, ultimately one is going to emerge with the authoritarian conclusions. The libertarian shell has fallen away, and we're left with the bedrock principles of compulsion and the subjection of human beings to a planning elite.

It doesn't have to be that way and some liberals have turned back in the other direction. It is my hope that those who have become disenchanted with the liberal formula will join with those of us who have criticized this approach for many years, and that between us we will be able to attack, in an intelligent way, the economic distresses which have afflicted our society and prevent the further erosion of our political system into authoritarian practice.

If such a united front can be, then I think there is some hope that emerging from this liberal twilight will be a more libertarian product than that I have been describing, and that those of us who are concerned for the future of our society can restore it to the ways of freedom intended for it by its founders.

B. A. Rogge

Adam Smith: 1776-1976

"To prohibit a great people [the American colonials] . . . from making all that they can of every part of their own produce, or from employing their [capital] and industry in the way that they judge most advantageous to themselves, is a manifest violation of the most sacred rights of mankind." Adam Smith, *The Wealth of Nations*, 1776.

"We hold these truths to be self-evident, that all men are created equal, that they are endowed by their Creator with certain unalienable Rights, that among these are Life, Liberty, and the Pursuit of Happiness." Thomas Jefferson, Declaration of Independence, 1776.

In these two passages, we find one of the common elements in the two significant bicentennials we celebrate this year. The common element is the conviction that man is endowed by a source greater than himself with certain

Adam Smith, *The Wealth of Nations*, Modern Library ed. (NY: Random House, 1937), p. 79. Dr. Rogge makes references to this edition throughout his paper.

natural and hence inalienable rights. This common element in the two bicentennials is one of the themes I shall develop in these comments of mine. But first let me hasten to admit that, in the households of the United States in 1976, the two bicentennials (the publication of *The Wealth of Nations* and the proclamation of the Declaration of Independence) are not held in equal awareness or veneration, nor does Adam Smith's name compete for the attention of the young with that of Thomas Jefferson. Yet it is my firm conviction that the members of our own society (and in fact of all societies based on the concept of freedom under law) must look to Smith as well as to Jefferson (and his fellow founding fathers) to fully understand our goodly heritage of freedom with order.

Here, as in all matters of judgment, I admit to bias. Adam Smith is generally known as the father of economics, the field of study which is also my own. Moreover, Smith's brand of economics, carrying the trademarks of voluntary exchange, freedom in the marketplace and limited government, is also my brand of economics—Brand X though it may have become in today's intellectual marketplace. Finally, I believe Adam Smith not only to have been possessed of true wisdom about the nature and possibilities of the human condition but also to have been possessed of a capacity to communicate those ideas with great clarity and great style. In other words, I am an admitted, card-carrying Adam Smith buff.

With no embarrassment, I admit that I hope through these words to encourage some of you who may now know little of Smith and his work to come to want to know more. Even for those who bring to their studies of Smith a presupposition against his strong free market policy position, there is something to be gained. His writing is free of that obscurantism, technical jargon and complicated mathematics that distinguish most modern materials in economics. In Smith's writings, the case for what might be roughly called "capitalism" is put in so clear and straightforward a fashion that it makes a useful stone against which even the convinced socialist can hone his own counter-arguments. Finally, no one who professes to understand even commonly well the course of events of these last two hundred years can afford to be ignorant of the influence on that course of events of the ideas of Adam Smith, whether they have been proven right or wrong. In the words of the historian, Henry Thomas Buckle, in his *The History of Civilization*, published in the middle of the last century: "In the year 1776, Adam Smith published his *Wealth of Nations*; which, looking at its ultimate results, is probably the most important book that has ever been written . . . ." (p. 122). Even a true Smith buff may be at least mildly embarrassed by this claim, but that his ideas did have consequences no one can really doubt.

Who was this man, what did he have to say in 1776 and how, if at all, is his thinking relevant to the world of 1976? Adam Smith was born in Kircaldy, Scotland, in 1723 and died in Edinburgh, Scotland, in 1790. In between he lived a life free of scandal, wife or children, great incident and severe disappointment. He was a student (at Glasgow and Oxford), a teacher (at Glasgow and Edinburgh) and a scholar, and his friends were not only students, teachers and scholars—but also artists, writers, businessmen and men of affairs. In a sense, though, he was the true "spectator"of the human scene, involved in that scene, yes, but always capable of detached analysis and appraisal of everything that came within his view.

Curiously enough, he was to use the concept of the "impartial spectator" as a rough synonym for what we term the human conscience in his first book, *The Theory of Moral Sentiments*. In fact, Smith published but two books in his lifetime, a record that would cost him his position on the faculty of almost any college or university of presumption in today's "publish or perish" world.

My intent here is to concentrate on Smith's words and ideas and on their usefulness (if any) in interpreting the modern scene. Those of you who wish to know more of Smith's life or of the intellectual influences that shaped his thinking or of his weaknesses and strengths as a pure technician in the science of economics will need to look elsewhere.

My plan is as follows: First, to present in concise form what I see as Smith's view of the social order. Next, to identify the ways in which he applied this view to the world of his day, particularly the British treatment of the American colonies. Finally, to identify those ways in which it seems to me that Smith speaks most directly to the problems and possibilities of today's world.

Section I - Smith's Basic Argument

We begin with what I believe to be the essence of the Smith argument—but first a word of preparation. Smith is known as the father of economics and the book whose bicentennial year we now celebrate has as its complete title, *An*

Inquiry into the Nature and Causes of the Wealth of Nations. The first sentence of Chapter I, Book I, reads as follows: "The greatest improvement in the productive powers of labour, and the greater part of the skill, dexterity, and judgment with which it is any where directed, or applied, seem to have been the effects of the division of labour." These substantial straws in the wind would seem to imply that we are about to grapple with a pure piece of economic analysis applied to the essentially vulgar question of how to multiply the quantity of "things" in a nation— and indeed Smith does have a kind word for those vulgar "things" when he writes that, "No society can surely be flourishing and happy, of which the greater part of the members are poor and miserable."

But to see Smith as nothing more that an early-day consultant on how to make everyone rich is to do him an injustice. Smith was first and foremost a professor of moral philosophy and his economic analysis was in a sense a by-product of his concern with such questions as the nature of the universe, the nature of man and the relationship of the individual to society.

When curiosity turns his attention to "the wealth of nations," he begins in effect by reaching into his philosopher's cupboard for the basic materials of his proposed studies. First and foremost he draws out his conviction that there exists a natural order in the universe which, if properly understood and lived in accordance with, tends to produce the "good." Coordinate with and deriving from this natural order is a set of natural rights of individuals (recall the phrasing of the opening passage from Smith— "the most sacred rights of mankind.") For a society to live in harmony with the natural order requires that it respect those "most sacred rights of mankind."

But what does all this have to do with getting more bread on the table? Comes now Smith, the eternal spectator, the observer of all that transpires around him, who is also curious as to what puts more bread on the table. His observations tell him very quickly that the wealth of a nation is primarily determined "by the skill, dexterity and judgment with which its labour is generally applied." But by what in turn are these determined? By two primary factors: (1) the extent to which the division of labor is carried in the society, and (2) the stock of capital available to the laborers.

But what forces give rise to or permit the division of labor and the accumulation of capital? Must it be the forces of the ruler, commanding one man to do this and another to do that and ordering all to go without so that the stock of capital may grow? Not at all, replies Smith, the observer-philosopher. *In the natural order of things,* man is so disposed to act as to promote these very ends without the necessity of external commands.

The division of labor finds some part of its initial support in man's natural instinct to truck and barter. More importantly, the apparent problem of securing each man's cooperation in serving the needs of others proves to be no problem at all. His cooperation is readily secured, not out of his benevolence, but out of his natural regard for his own interest. "It is not from the benevolence of the butcher, the brewer, or the baker, that we expect our dinner, but from their regard to their own self-interest."

Thus the seeds of the division of labor lie in the very nature of man, that is, in the natural order. In the same way, man's desire for improvement induces him to save and hence to accumulate the capital needed to add even further to the productivity of labor.

But how are the activities of all of these specialists coordinated, what assures that the various parts and processes will be brought together properly in time and place and quantity and quality and all other relevant attributes? In Smith's own words, "Observe the accommodation of the most common artificer or day-labourer in a civilised or thriving country, and you will perceive that the number of people of whose industry, a part has been employed in procuring him this accommodation, exceeds all computation." (p. 11) But what great force is to give order to the activities of this great number of persons that "exceeds all computation"? Surely here the offices of government must be required. Not at all, Smith replies; a spontaneous order emerges in the very nature of things, an order that arises out of the interaction in the marketplace between the two great forces of supply and demand.

If any one element in this complex chain comes to be in short supply, its price will rise and suppliers will be induced to bring more to the market; in cases of excess supply, the reverse. In this way, in Smith's words, "the quantity of every commodity brought to market naturally suits itself to the effectual demand." (p. 57)

The marketplace, then, as a spontaneously emerging and self-regulating process, is but the natural order at work in the ordering of economic life.

The pattern is now complete and he concludes as follows:

As every individual, therefore, endeavours as much as he can both to employ his capital in the support of industry, and so to direct that industry that its produce may be of the greatest value; every individual necessarily labours to render the annual revenues of the society as great as he can. He generally indeed neither intends to promote the public interest, nor knows by how much is he promoting it . . . . He intends only his own gain, and he is in this, as in many other cases, led by an invisible hand to promote an end which was no part of his intention. (p. 423)

Continuing with Smith's words:

All systems either of preference or of restraint, therefore, being thus completely taken away, the obvious and simple system of natural liberty establishes itself of its own accord. Every man, as long as he does not violate the laws of justice, is left perfectly free to pursue his own interest his own way, and to bring both his industry and capital into competition with those of any other man, or order of men. The sovereign is completely discharged from a duty, in the attempting to perform which he must always be exposed to innumerable delusions, and for the proper performance of which no human wisdom or knowledge could ever be sufficient; the duty of superintending the industry of private people, and of directing it towards the employments most suitable to the interest of the society. According to the system of natural liberty, the sovereign has only three duties to attend to; three duties of great importance, indeed, but plain and intelligible to common understandings: first, the duty of protecting the society from the violence and invasion of other independent societies; secondly, the duty of protecting, as far as possible, every member of the society from the injustice or oppression of every other member of it, or the duty of establishing an exact administration of justice; and, thirdly, the duty of erecting and maintaining certain public works and certain public institutions, which it can never be for the interest of any individual, or small number of individuals, to erect and maintain; because the profit could never repay the expence to any individual or small number of individuals, though it may frequently do much more than repay it to a great society. (p. 651)

Section II - Smith's Thinking Applied to the Problems of His Day

Here, with much of the detail omitted, is the Smithian system. In his own day, it led him to attack virtually all those actions of governments that restricted man's freedom in economic life, i.e., which constricted the extent of the market and hence the division of labor, or worked against the natural tendency to the accumulation of capital. The state-supported activities he attacked ranged from the regulations of the medieval guilds, to the long apprenticeships required of many artisans, to the grants of special privileges (usually grants of monopoly power) to individuals or groups for various goods or services or even whole geographic areas, to the profligate spending of governments, to all of the regulations of economic practice that were a part of the mercantilist position of the governments of the day.

In a very real sense, *The Wealth of Nations* can be viewed as an attack on the prevailing economic philosophy and practice of the author's day—an untidy collection of ideas and actions identified as mercantilism. Mercantilism, as you know, was associated with the more powerful nation-states of seventeenth and eighteenth century Europe, with England, France, Spain, Portugal and Holland. Its primary purpose was to enhance the power and wealth of the nation, whether led by a king or a Cromwell or a Parliament. The techniques were those of control—control not only of foreign trade (for the purpose of assuring a favorable balance of trade), control not only of colonies around the world, but control of most aspects of domestic economic life as well.

Smith argued that such controls were in fact directly opposed to the ultimate ends they were designed to serve. Thus, not only were the economic controls placed on her American colonies "a manifest violation of the most sacred rights of mankind," but moreover, "under the present system of management Great Britain derives nothing but loss from the dominion which she assumes over her colonies." (p. 581)

And in another passage: "It is not very difficult to determine who have been the contrivers of this whole mercantile system: not the consumers, we may believe, whose interests have been entirely neglected; but the producers, whose interest has been so carefully attended to . . . ." (p. 626)

What were his proposals for the British colonies? Radical ones indeed. His first was "that Great Britain should voluntarily give up all authority over her colonies, and leave them to elect their own magistrates, to enact their own laws, and to make peace and war as they might think proper." (p. 581) However, he admitted that this was "to propose such a measure as never was and never will be adopted, by any nation in the world." Why not? Not because such an action wouldn't be beneficial to the interests of the society but because it would be "mortifying to the pride" and because it would deprive the *rulers* "of the disposal of many places of trust and profit, of many opportunities of acquiring wealth and distinction, which the possession of the most turbulent, and, to the great body of the people, the most unprofitable province seldom fails to afford." (p. 582) Yet he noted that in the unlikely event the rulers of Great Britain were to follow his advice, mother country and former colonies could part as "good friends," bound together by "natural affection."

His next and somewhat less sweeping proposal was that Great Britain give the colonies direct representation in Parliament:

> If to each colony, which should detach itself from the general confederacy, Great Britain should allow such a number of representatives as suited the proportion of what it contributed to the public revenue of the empire, in consequence of its being subjected to the same taxes, and in compensation admitted to the same freedom of trade with its fellow-subjects at home; the number of its representatives to be augmented as the proportion of its contribution might afterwards augment; a new method of acquiring importance, a new and more dazzling object of ambition would be presented to the leading men of each colony. Instead of piddling for the little prizes which are to be found in what may be called the paltry raffle of colony faction; they might then hope, from the presumption which men naturally have in their own ability and good fortune, to draw some of the great prizes which sometimes come from the wheel of the great state lottery of British politics. (p. 587)

He goes on to argue that unless this or some other method is found of "preserving the importance and of gratifying the ambition of the leading men of America, it is not very probable that they will ever voluntarily submit to us." Moreover (in a phrase of shrewd prophecy), "they are very weak who flatter themselves that, in the state to which things have come, our colonies will be easily conquered by force alone." (p. 587)

"From shopkeepers, tradesmen, and attornies, they are become statesmen and legislators, and are employed in contriving a new form of government for an extensive empire, which, they flatter themselves, will become, and which, indeed, seems very likely to become, one of the greatest and most formidable that ever was in the world." (pp. 587-8)

These words could have been written no later than 1775 and speak well, at the very least, of Smith's powers of prophecy. Would Sam Adams, if offered a seat in the British Parliament, have quickly forsaken his hawkish ways and prepared for a journey to London? No one can say, and, in any case, the course of events was not to grant him that option.

In concluding this section, I wish to point out that Smith's handling of the colonial question was in full accord with and, in fact, derived directly from his general philosophy of free peoples, free economies and free societies. One of Smith's remarkable characteristics was his consistency, his predictability. I mean by this if one were to know only his general framework, one could predict his response to most questions of applied policy with astonishing accuracy.

Take another famous example (which I believe to have great relevance to today's world of education): his handling of the proper organization of colleges and universities. His own experience at Oxford had not been a particularly happy one; as he was to write many years later, "In the university of Oxford, the greater part of the professors have . . . given up altogether even the pretence of teaching." (p. 718)

But why should this be? The source of the problem is to be found in the *endowments* of the institutions of learning. "The endowments of schools and colleges have necessarily diminished more or less the necessity of application in the teachers. Their subsistence, so far as it arises from their salaries, is evidently derived from a fund altogether independent of their success and reputation in their particular professions." (p. 717)

He continues: "It is the interest of every man to live as much at his ease as he can; and if his emoluments are to be precisely the same, whether he does or does not perform some very laborious duty it is his interest ... either to neglect it altogether [or] ... to perform it in as careless and slovenly a matter as ... authority will permit." (p. 718)

In a sentence prophetic of the publishing-consulting-public-speech-making world (*Mea Culpa!*) of the modern academician, he continues: "If he is naturally active and has a love of labour, it is his interest to employ that activity in any way, from which he can derive some advantage, rather than in the performance of his duty, from which he can derive none."

He offers some tongue-in-cheek advice to teachers on how to *seem* to be giving a lecture but with minimal or no effort, and comments (no doubt with some remembered bitterness of his student days) "that the discipline of the college may enable [the teacher] to force all his pupils to the most regular attendance upon this sham-lecture, and to maintain the most decent and respectful behavior during the whole time of the performance." He concludes that, "The discipline of colleges and universities is in general contrived, not for the benefit of the students, but for the interest, or more properly speaking, for the ease of the masters." The policy inference is clear, even if frightening to those of us who now inhabit the college world of endowed or tax-paid ease: Let the income of the teacher be determined by the fees voluntarily paid by the student.

In the same way, he proposes that all of his third-function-of-government activities be financed as much as possible by fees paid by those who benefit directly from those activities. "Public services are never better performed than when their reward comes only in consequence of their being performed and is proportioned to the diligence employed in performing them." (p. 678) Thus, "the whole expense of justice might easily be defrayed by the fees of court . . . a highway, a bridge, a navigable canal . . . may in most cases be both made and maintained by a small toll upon the carriages which make use of them, a harbour by a moderate port duty. The post-office, over beyond defraying its own expense, affords in almost all countries a very considerable revenue to the sovereign." (p. 682) Alas, even Adam Smith was not always blessed with perfect foresight. However, he was a good believer in the idea of federalism. "Public works . . . of which the conveniency is nearly confined to some particular place or district, are always better maintained by a local or provincial revenue, under the management of a local and provincial administration, than by the general revenue of the state." (p. 689)

Section III - Is Smith Still Relevant?

The question now before us is whether Smith's work is of only antiquarian interest to those of us who inhabit the world of 1976—or does it have some continuing relevance? I intend to argue that Smith does indeed provide us with most useful insights into our own problems and with those insights often so phrased as to make them at least the equal in power of persuasion of any later versions of the same thinking. I offer up now for your examination a series of examples, presented in no particular order.

To those who call for the businessman (or others) to act less on self-interest and more on the desire to serve others, he answers: "I have never known much good done by those who affected to trade for the public good. It is an affectation, indeed, not very common among merchants, and very few words need be employed in dissuading them from it." (p. 423)

To those who are now calling for some kind of national economic plan for the United States, he responds:

What is the species of domestic industry which his capital can employ, and of which the produce is likely to be of the greatest value, every individual, it is evident, can, in his local situation, judge much better than any statesman or lawgiver can do for him. The statesman, who should attempt to direct private people in what manner they ought to employ their capitals, would not only load himself with a most unnecessary attention, but assume an authority which could safely be trusted, not only to no single person, but to no council or senate whatever, and which would nowhere be so dangerous as in the hands of a man who had folly and presumption enough to fancy himself fit to exercise it. (p. 423)

To those special interests who demand protection from goods produced in other countries: "By means of glasses, hotbeds and hotwalls, very good grapes can be raised in Scotland, and very good wines too can be made of them *at about thirty times the expence* from which at least equally good can be brought from foreign countries. Would it be a reasonable law to prohibit the importation of all foreign wines, merely to encourage the making of claret and burgundy in Scotland?" (p. 425)

To those who demand protection from foreign goods on the general grounds of securing or maintaining a stock of gold and silver: "A country that has the wherewithal to buy wine, will always get the wine which it has occasion for; and a country that has wherewithal to buy gold and silver, will never be in want of those metals." (p. 403) "To attempt to increase the wealth of any country, either by introducing, or by detaining in it an unnecessary quantity of gold and silver, is as absurd as it would be to attempt to increase the good cheer of private families, by obliging them to keep an unnecessary number of kitchen utensils." (p. 408)

To the tendency of governors and governments to reduce the purchasing power of the money (that is, to produce inflation):

> For in every country of the world, I believe, the avarice and injustice of princes and sovereign states, abusing the confidence of their subjects, have by degrees diminished the real quantity of metal, which had been originally contained in their coins. The Roman As, in the latter ages of the Republic, was reduced to the twenty-fourth part of its original value.... The English pound and penny contain at present about a third only; the Scots pounds and penny about a thirty-sixth; and the French pound and penny about a sixty-sixth part of their original value .... Such operations have always proved favorable to the debtor, and ruinous to the creditor, and have sometimes produced a greater and more universal revolution in the fortunes of private persons, than could have been occasioned by a very great public calamity. (pp. 27-8)

On the behavior of organizations of workers: "Their usual pretences are sometimes the high price of provisions;

sometimes the great profit which their masters make by their work. . . . Their combinations . . . are always abundantly heard of. In order to bring the point to a speedy decision, they have always recourse to the loudest clamour, and sometimes to the most shocking violence and outrage." (p. 67)

In fact, though, Smith's sympathies were with the workers (as against the masters) and he was pleased with what he observed to be the improvement in the lot of the common worker in the England of his day. "Compared indeed with the more extravagant luxury of the great, his accommodation must no doubt appear extremely simple and easy; and yet it may be true, perhaps, that the accommodation of an European prince does not always so much exceed that of an industrious and frugal peasant, as the accommodation of the latter exceeds that of many an African king, the absolute master of the lives and liberties of ten thousand naked savages." (p. 12)

"The common complaint that luxury extends itself even to the lowest ranks of the people, and that the labouring poor will not now be contented with the same food, clothing and lodging which satisfied them in former times, may convince us that it is not the money price of labour only, but its real recompence which has augmented." (p. 78)

Moreover, he argued against the idea that hard-driven workers would produce more than those more humanely treated: "If masters would always listen to the dictates of reason and humanity, they have frequently occasion rather to moderate, than to animate the application of many of their workmen. It will be found, I believe, in every sort of trade, that the man who works so moderately, as to be able to work constantly, not only preserves his health the longest, but, in the course of the year, executes the greatest quantity of work." (p. 82)

To the argument that the workman (and those who use his services) must be protected by apprenticeships, licensing, or wage-setting by law, he responds:

> The property which every man has in his own labour, as it is the original foundation of all other property, so it is the most sacred and inviolable. The patrimony of a poor man lies in the strength and dexterity of his hands; and to hinder him from employing this strength and dexterity in what manner he thinks proper without injury to his neighbour, is a plain violation of this most sacred property. It is a manifest encroachment upon the just liberty both of the workman, and of those who might be disposed to employ him. As it hinders the one from working at what he thinks proper, so it hinders the others from employing whom they think proper. To judge whether he is fit to be employed, may surely be trusted to the discretion of the employers whose interest it so much concerns. The affected anxiety of the lawgiver lest they should employ an improper person, is evidently as impertinent as it is oppressive. (pp. 121-2)

To the argument that guilds or unions are necessary to quality workmanship, he replies in the negative: "If you would have your work tolerably executed, it must be done in the suburbs, where the workmen, having no exclusive privilege, have nothing but their character to depend upon, and you must then smuggle it into the town as well as you can." (p. 129)

But his criticism of some practices of workmen should not be taken to mean that he was uncritical of the businessman or merchant. To many of both the initiated and the uninitiated, Adam Smith is seen as a spokesman for the business interest. Thus, for reasons that can only be guessed at, when The Modern Library edition of *The Wealth of Nations* was published in 1937, it included an introduction by Max Lerner, then editor of *The Nation*. In his introduction, Lerner approvingly quotes Harold Laski's statement about Smith: "To have their [the businessmen's] own longings elevated to the dignity of a natural law was to provide them with a driving force that had never before been so powerful .... With Adam Smith the practical maxims of business enterprise achieved the status of a theology." (p. ix)

Lerner goes on to add that Smith "was an unconscious mercenary in the service of a rising capitalist class. ... He gave a new dignity to greed and a new sanctification of the predatory impulses .... He rationalized the economic interests of the class that was coming to power ...." (pp. ix-x)

Even though Lerner admits that "Smith's doctrine has been twisted in ways he would not have approved," the damage is already done and Smith is confirmed again in the mind of the reading public as the puppet of the bourgeois business interest—a view of him that continues to this day to color the thinking of those who might otherwise learn from him.

Compare this view of Smith with these words in which he describes the proper attitude of the society to proposals for legislation coming from businessmen (and which serves equally well to answer those today who believe that we can best solve our problems by turning over our economic decision-making to good, experienced, competent leaders of business): "The proposal of any new law or regulation which comes from this order [the businessmen] ought always to be listened to with great precaution, and ought never to be adopted till after having been long and carefully examined, not only with the most scrupulous, but with the most suspicious attention. It comes from an order of men, whose interest is never exactly the same with that of the public, who have generally an interest to deceive and even to oppress the public, and who accordingly have, upon many occasions, both deceived and oppressed it." (p. 250)

Nor is Smith at all unaware of the ancient (and modern) propensity of businessmen as well as others to attempt to combine to restrict competition. In a famous passage he writes that, "People of the same trade seldom meet together, even for merriment and diversion, but the conversation ends in a conspiracy against the public, or in some contrivance to raise prices." (p. 128)

At the same time, his recommendations for dealing with such cases seem to me to reflect greater wisdom than our policies of today. He continues from the statement above: "It is impossible indeed to prevent such meetings, by any law which either could be executed, or would be consistent with liberty and justice. But though the law cannot hinder people of the same trade from sometimes assembling together, it ought to do nothing to facilitate such assemblies; much less to render them necessary." (p. 128)

But wouldn't such a policy leave the public to the none-too-tender mercies of the conspirators? Not at all, replies Smith. Why not? Because in the absence of government backing, such conspiracies do not survive. "In a free trade an effectual combination cannot be established but by the unanimous consent of every single trader, and it cannot last longer than every single trader continues of the same mind. The majority of a corporation [i.e., of a government-granted monopoly power to a group of traders] can enact a by-law with proper penalties, which will limit the competition more effectually and more durably than any voluntary combination whatever." (p. 129)

As a matter of fact, in this whole area of competition and monopoly, it seems to me that Smith speaks with more wisdom than most modern economists and most of the associated legislation. Smith creates no unattainable ideal of "perfect competition" as a bench mark for use in appraisal and policy-making. Rather he argues that "all systems either of preference or of restraint ... being thus completely taken away [that is, all government interventionist action removed from the marketplace] the obvious and simple system of natural liberty establishes itself of its own accord." (p. 651)

In other words, all that governments must do to see that competition (i.e., the open marketplace) prevails is *not* to create monopoly. Competition does not need to be created or protected or restored—it inheres in the natural order of things and in the very nature of man. I believe this to have been true in 1776 and to be equally true in 1976. The technological changes of the last two hundred years have served only to make the competitive process *more* intense and to ensure the even quicker demise of the firm that doesn't maintain a perpetual effort to serve its customers better.

But enough of the examples. If you are not yet persuaded of Smith's continuing relevance, a further parade of cases is not likely to be useful. God knows I may be in error, but I am convinced that Smith is not only relevant today but that his insight and wisdom, if applied to today's world, would yield not only a freer but a more productive and equitable set of economic arrangements than if we applied a mixture of what was thought to be the best of contemporary thought.

This does not mean that I have no quarrels with Smith: his third function of government seems to me to be a Pandora's Box; his handling of the theory of value, of what determines the ratio of exchange among goods and services, seems to me to be importantly in error, etc.

At the same time, I yield to no one in my admiration for his wisdom and for his magnificent contribution to our understanding of ourselves and of our institutions, in the form particularly of this book whose bicentenary year of publication we celebrate this year. It was from this book that such disparate types as William Pitt and Edmund Burke in England and Alexander Hamilton and John Adams in this country admitted having drawn some part of their own thinking on political economy. It is my reasoned conviction that the well-being of every society in the modern world would be at a significantly higher level if more of those in leadership roles in our societies of today were to be reading *The Wealth of Nations* rather than the modern works from which they draw their tragically mistaken policy advice.

To those who argue that no nation in the world is ever likely to follow Smith's advice in every detail, and that hence we can regard that advice as essentially irrelevant, I offer Smith's own assurance that nothing like absolute purity is required for the general system of natural liberty to work its wonders. "If a nation could not prosper without the enjoyment of perfect liberty and perfect justice, there is not in the world a nation which could ever have prospered. In the political body, however, the wisdom of nature has fortunately made ample provision for remedying many of the bad effects of the folly and injustice of man; in the same manner as it has done in the natural body, for remedying those of his sloth and intemperance." (p. 638)

In another passage, he argues that each man's attempt to better his own condition "frequently restores health and vigour to the constitution, in spite, not only of the disease, but of the absurd prescriptions of the doctor." (p. 326)

In a word, there is usually still time for a society to mend its ways if the will but exists. But of course the will to freedom within each individual and within a society is always confronting its enemy in the form of the will to control.

I close now with a final offering of the wisdom of Adam Smith, this on the inherent error in *all* systems of control and this one coming not from *The Wealth of Nations* but from his first book, *The Theory of Moral Sentiments*.

> The man of system, is apt to be very wise in his own conceit, and is often so enamoured with the supposed beauty of his own ideal plan of government, that he cannot suffer the smallest deviation from any part of it. He goes on to establish it completely and in all its parts, without any regard either to the great interests or to the strong prejudices which may oppose it: he seems to imagine that he can arrange the different members of a great society with as much ease as the hand arranges the different pieces upon a chess-board; he does not consider that the pieces upon the chess-board have no other principle of motion besides that which the hand impresses upon them; but that, in the great chess-board of human society, every single piece has a principle of motion of its own, altogether different from that which the legislature might choose to impress upon

it. If those two principles coincide and act in the same direction, the game of human society will go on easily and harmoniously, and is very likely to be happy and successful. If they are opposite or different, the game will go on miserably, and the society must be at all times in the highest degree of disorder. (pp. 342-3)

Gottfried Dietze

Hayek and the Rule of Law

Back in 1967, when I was going to an ISI seminar at the University of Virginia, I saw an old gentleman huddled up in his chair at the airport in Washington and recognized him as Dr. Ludwig von Mises. I was delighted to hear that he was also going to Charlottesville. On our way, we talked a great deal about Hayek's *Constitution of Liberty*. Dr. von Mises was very much interested in what Hayek had to say about the rule of law. So I thought this was a proper topic to suggest for a Mises lecture.

The last lecture in this series was given by my good friend, Benjamin Rogge, on Adam Smith. Smith is known mainly as a founder of the science of political economy, as an advocate of free enterprise. He also is a political philosopher and his values are similar to those of Friedrich von Hayek. Smith was a firm believer in freedom. One of his main achievements was the liberation of the individual from the government, the emancipation of nations from mercantilism. However, he realized that freedom should exist with measure. Therefore, he was an advocate of the rule of law. To Smith, the rule of law mainly meant two things: the absence of governmental despotism and the protection of the individual from his fellow men. It implied freedom under law. Whereas that government is best that governs least, there must be a government which protects one citizen from the other. The rule of law for Adam Smith implied a minimum of governmental regulation as well as the enforcement of the laws by the government. In a liberal state, there should be as little legal interference with the freedom of the individual as possible. However, the few laws that can be found in it were to be strictly enforced; otherwise, a liberal state would degenerate into anarchy.

Hayek's concept of the rule of law is quite similar. In the age of absolute monarchy and mercantilism, Adam Smith was one of the founders of liberalism, who, like Montesquieu, initiated the modern liberal era. In view of the growing collectivism, Hayek perhaps is one of the last great liberals. His political, economic and legal thought combine the wisdom of Montesquieu and Smith. Hayek's predominant value is, I think, measured freedom. Smithian measure is evident in his *Wealth of Nations,* the bicentennial of which we celebrate on March 9, and in *The Theory of Moral Sentiments.* Hayek significantly often cites mottoes from Goethe, a humanist of measure. As it did for Smith, the rule of law for Hayek implies two kinds of legal measure: the right amount of freedom from the government, and the maintenance of the liberal order through the strict enforcement of the laws.

The idea of freedom stands in the foreground of Hayek's

legal and political thought. Years ago, when quite a few people had serious doubts about the survival of freedom, intellectual leaders were asked how they evaluated its chances. Hayek was one of the few who said that freedom would survive. He stated that people never have been willing to be without freedom and to put up with despotism for a long time. The idea of freedom is evident in all of his writings since he published *The Road to Serfdom* in 1944. A road to serfdom, by definition, is one away from freedom. In this famous book, Hayek explained how Germany moved away from a belief in liberty through the acceptance of more or less socialist doctrines. Hayek weakened a thesis that was quite current at that time outside of Germany, namely, that the Third Reich was due to the fact that big business and the big landowners, the *Junkers*, had paved the way for Hitler. Actually the Weimar Republic, with its emphasis upon social rights, upon the concentration of power in the central government, and upon a strong executive, in a way served despotic features to Hitler on a platter. *The Road to Serfdom* was followed, in 1960, by *The Constitution of Liberty*. In this book, Hayek talks about his ideal form of government and suggests what can be done to guarantee a maximum of freedom. The predominance of freedom is also evident in the title of his last work, *Law, Legislation and Liberty*, a more practical study written to aid in realizing the ideals of *The Constitution of Liberty*.

An important distinction is suggested in the title *Law, Legislation and Liberty*, reflecting Hayek's ideas on the rule of law. Liberty is the end, law a means for its achievement. Legislation can be a means to secure liberty, but being distinguished from law, it also can do away with liberty. Here we have what I think are Hayek's two concepts of the rule of law. The term "rule of law" basically can mean two things. On the one hand, it prescribes the restriction of the government through the law. This classic liberal concept amounts to constitutionalism, implying the limitation of the government for the sake of the freedom of the individual. On the other hand, the rule of law can mean the rule of the laws, regulations, and commands that are made by any particular government at any particular time—all of which can potentially oppress rather than emancipate the individual.

It is obvious that Hayek favors the former concept of the rule of law. For him, law basically implies a restriction of the government. He traces the development of this concept from ancient Greece on, through the common law tradition to our day. Outstanding steps in this development are the Magna Charta, the Petition of Right, the Bill of Rights, and the great democratic revolutions in England, America and France. Important also is its evolution in Germany, the development of the *Rechtsstaat*. This concept of the rule of law provides for a government of law and not of men. James Harrington believed in it, and later A. V. Dicey, who, in his *Law of the Constitution*, describes the English constitutional heritage.

Hayek is of the opinion that this concept of the rule of law has come about gradually. In other words, constitutionalism basically is reflected in the English common law tradition. Here again, Hayek is in agreement with Adam Smith. Smith's "great society" is rather different from Lyndon Johnson's. It is a society of free and responsible individuals who are not disturbed by government planning. It lives under a law that has come about through spontaneous custom. If people voluntarily adopt certain customs and agree that these customs are worth having and for that reason transmute them into laws, and accept these laws for generations, such laws must be good laws favoring freedom. The spontaneous, customary law thus comes close to Smithian justice, some kind of natural justice that has the blessings of God.

From this kind of law Hayek distinguishes the law made on the spur of the moment, indicated by Thomas Paine's statement that a constitution does not exist unless one can put it into one's pocket. The implication of this statement is that law does not exist unless it is written down. Paine's kind of law is similar to that advocated during the American Revolution by Benjamin Hichborn. Asked in the 1770s what freedom is, Hichborn said that it is the right of the ruling majority to do whatever it pleases at any time and to enact its wishes into law. He thus said something similar to what had been stated by James I; namely, that whatever pleases the prince at any particular moment shall have the force of the law. Just as the author on the divine right of kings had maintained that the voice of the king is the voice of God, Hichborn in a democratic atmosphere maintained that the voice of the people is the voice of God, an idea that was entertained also during the French Revolution. Hayek dislikes this kind of spontaneous law. Law should grow gradually rather than be made on the spur of the moment. Hayek distinguishes between a law that is made slowly and one that is made quickly. He considers the latter dangerous because it can actually annihilate the former. The law made by an oppressive majority can eliminate the slowly grown law that provides for freedom just as much as a law decreed by a despot. Hayek entertains strong fears about legislation. He bewails that legislation has increasingly superseded customary law, and has been detrimental to freedom.

We know, of course, that in the nineteenth and early twentieth century, legislation was not so bad. In a large measure, it promoted freedom. Liberty was in the air, partly due to the impact of Adam Smith's *The Wealth of Nations.* Legislators emphasized the importance of freedom and of laissez faire. A study of the great codifications adopted during that time, such as the Napoleonic codes of the first decade of the nineteenth century, the German codes adopted after unification in 1871, and the civil code of Switzerland, easily reveals that these laws are individualistic and in a way complement customary law favoring liberty. But then things changed. In the twentieth century legislation became oppressive. Laws made by the government, whether it was the government of one man, or a few, or of the many, in a large measure restricted freedom.

Hayek describes, with regrets, how the traditional constitutionalist concept of the rule of law with its liberal contents became increasingly formalized. Whereas it formerly was said that under the rule of law the government cannot interfere in the freedom of the individual, now it was asserted that the rule of law merely implied the observance of certain forms. In other words, the government could interfere as much into the freedom of the individual as it wanted to, provided it did so under the forms prescribed by the law. If there prevailed nationalistic views, the government could interfere with the freedom of the individual on the basis of law for the sake of nationalism. If socialistic views were prevailing, the rulers could interfere with freedom on the basis of socialistic law. They could do so on the basis of communist as well as fascist law. In distinction to Hayek, communist, fascist, socialist and nationalist jurists felt that all this was compatible with the rule of law.

There is, then, a dichotomy in the law. On the one hand, it can be conducive to freedom. On the other hand, it can be detrimental to it. And the chances that law will be detrimental to freedom increase with the increase of legislation, and of administrative decrees, rules and regulations made on the basis of legislative delegations of power to administrative officials.

The fact that to Hayek the rule of law implies limitations upon the government does not mean that he would reject government. Skeptical as he is toward governmental power, he favors governmental authority whenever it is appropriate, be it reflected in the making or in the execution of the laws.

Hayek's skepticism toward legislation must not conceal the fact that he attributes important functions to it. While a particular enactment can infringe upon the rule of law, it must not do so. As long as legislation establishes general rules and is not either directly aimed at particular people or at enabling anybody to use the coercive power of the state for the purpose of such discrimination, it is compatible with the rule of law. Legislation, together with adjudication, can approach the ideal of the rule of law. This is evident when Hayek discusses the generality, equality and certainty of the law, the separation of powers, administrative discretion, legislation and policy. Legislative acts can decide the use of the means which are put at the state's disposal and are in effect orders to its servants. While such acts are not generally valid for everybody, there are on the other hand legislative acts which constitute general rules. This kind of legislation is in conformity with the rule of law and is likely to be conducive to the freedom of the individual. The same applies to legislation that binds the administration. The legislature may well delegate powers to administrators in order that the latter may make rules for the protection of the individual. Legislation has the important function of adding the contributions of speculative thinkers, after they have passed through a long process of selection and modification in the course of time, to the body of the law.

The title of Hayek's last work, *Law, Legislation and Liberty,* shows a fundamental distinction between law and legislation. Its first volume, *Rules and Order,* devotes a chapter to "Nomos: The Law of Liberty," and one to "Thesis: The Law of Legislation." The latter appears to be at variance with the law of liberty. Yet in spite of all emphasis upon the threat of legislation to freedom, Hayek, in a chapter on the changing concept of the law, shows why grown law requires correction by legislation. He thus admits the value of legislation in a way that reminds us of the admission, centuries ago, of the value of equity as a corrective of the common law.

The need for legislation follows from various considerations. One is the slow and gradual process of judicial development, which precludes a rapid adaptation of the law to wholly new circumstances. The legislature must become

active here because the judges should use restraint in
reversing judicial development which has already taken
place and is then seen to have undesirable consequences or
to be downright wrong. Hayek also stresses the liberating
effect of legislation. Better than judicial decisions, legislation may do away with injustices which are due to the fact
"that the development of the law has lain in the hands of
members of a particular class whose traditional views made
them regard as just what could not meet the more general
requirements of justice." Thus, legislation can be an essential support of liberalism.

Hayek goes further than maintaining that the law of the
state can aid the rule of law. To him, the existence of state
law is a prerequisite for that rule and the freedom it
protects.

The rule of law does not merely imply a restriction of
the government for the sake of the individual through the
law. Law implies sanction by the government vis-à-vis individuals. So does "rule." Law being an ethical minimum, it
is the very essence of that minimum that it is enforceable.
In view of the fact that all law in one way or another
measures and restricts, law implies the absence of license.
Although freedom is the predominant value in Hayek's
social thought, Hayek is not inclined toward anarchy. He
wants freedom under law. True freedom is something tangible which cannot exist without the definition and protection
of the laws. While the law of the state, just as the empire of
men of which Harrington spoke, can and does infringe upon
the freedom of the individual, that freedom—i. e., what is
recognized of it in society—is protected by virtue of the
law. It is the law which transforms parts of the general,

vague, and intangible concept of freedom into specific and clearly defined tangible rights of the individual. As the title of his book shows, Hayek does not just believe in liberty. He believes in the *constitution* of liberty. He prefers a constituted liberty over a non-constituted one, even though the former may not be a transmutation into reality of freedom in its totality. Hayek favors a liberal constitution, a liberal order. To him, order is the prerequisite for freedom. While freedom is the great ideal that hovers over the legal order and always prompts that order to become more free, the legal order is the—if only partial—realization of the ideal. The genuine liberal realizes that it is reasonable to accept the authority of the state, while always being wary of its power. *Potestas* is dangerous. *Auctoritas* is necessary.

Hayek's admission of the necessity of authority in a liberal state makes him reluctant to want radical change. For the sake of order, he is willing to make compromises at the cost of liberty, realizing that liberty, to be useful to men, must be protected by a legal order.

Already in *The Road to Serfdom,* Hayek states that within the known rules of the game the individual is free to pursue his personal ends and desires: known rules can restrict freedom. In 1953, he approves of Louis Philippe's expressing ideas of Benjamin Constant, according to which liberty exists only under the law, and everybody must do what the law requires. His third Cairo lecture, entitled "The Safeguards of Individual Liberty," is given under Ortega's motto, "Order is not a pressure imposed upon society from without, but an equilibrium which is set up from within." He first discusses "Law and Order" as a prerequisite for liberty, making it plain that order does not exist merely as a result of human design, but also as a result of human action. In *The Constitution of Liberty,* Hayek devotes a chapter to "Responsibility and Freedom," writing: "Liberty and responsibility are inseparable. A free society will not function or maintain itself unless its members regard it as right that each individual occupy the position that results from his action and accept it as due to his own action. Though it can offer to the individual only changes and though the outcome of his efforts will depend on innumerable accidents, it forcefully directs his attention to those circumstances that he can control as if they were the only ones that mattered." The liberal society "forcefully directs" through the enforcement of its laws, which the responsible individual respects. He continues with regrets: "This belief in individual responsibility, which has always been strong when people firmly believed in individual freedom, has markedly declined, together with the esteem for freedom. Responsibility has become an unpopular concept, a word that experienced speakers or writers avoid because of the obvious boredom or animosity with which it is received by a generation that dislikes all moralizing." While responsibility means an unceasing task, a discipline that man must impose upon himself if he is to achieve his aims, it implies responsibility toward others. It means obedience to the laws. The latter idea is elaborated in the chapter, "Coercion and the State." Of his last work, finally, Hayek says: "The central concept around which the discussion of this book will turn is that of order .... Order is an indispensable concept .... We cannot do without it."

Hayek believes that a spontaneous order is more conducive to liberty than an imposed one. Yet for the sake of order, he refrains from denying that the latter and its laws should be complied with. The same applies to the law that comes about through evolution and one that is the result of "reason," the law produced by human action and one produced by human design. Hayek bewails that during the last generations, private law has been increasingly replaced by public law, the former aiding, the latter threatening, liberty. Yet he does not urge disobedience to public law. He complains that law in the sense of general rules is being challenged by law in the sense of organizational orders. Yet, while he sees the latter as a danger to liberty, he does not want it disobeyed. He feels that law based upon just principles is better for freedom than law based upon expediency. However, the latter must be obeyed. He distinguishes between *nomos,* the law of liberty, and *thesis*, the law of legislation. There is no doubt about the former's greater liberal content. But Hayek wants the latter to be complied with all the same.

Hayek's emphasis on order, his willingness to compromise at the cost of freedom, does not necessarily compromise freedom. On the contrary, it serves liberty by securing its protection through laws. Laws reflect reason. "Though the sentiments which are expressed in such terms as the 'dignity of man' and the 'beauty of liberty' are noble and praiseworthy, they can have no place in an attempt at rational persuasion," he writes in the introduction to *The Constitution of Liberty.* He wants to promote freedom rationally through the law, the enforceable and enforced law of the state. In doing so, the unrepentant Old Whig is an adamant advocate of law and order. He follows those who before him belived in the rule of law with its maximal realization of liberty. To Hayek, freedom ought to be the spirit of the laws. And the laws alone can transform that spirit into true rights.

Hayek's ideas on the rule of law reveal him as a man of measure.

As we are close to the bicentennial of the publication of *The Wealth of Nations*, Hayek's legal thoughts remind us not only of Montesquieu. They also let us think of Adam Smith. The measure implied in the balance of powers made the Frenchman, often considered the father of constitutionalism, famous. Measure is also characteristic of the Scotsman, in whom many see the founder of economic liberalism. Like Hayek, Smith saw, as did Montesquieu, in the rule of law a means for the promotion of freedom. For Smith, justice implied the liberation of man from private as well as public oppression. Yet, in spite of his emphasis upon liberty, Smith is careful not to tend toward anarchy. He is convinced that the wealth of nations can be increased by the freedom of the individual rather than by his regulation and regimentation. At the same time, he admits controls here and there for what he considers the good of the society and its members. And he leaves no doubt that justice implies the protection of citizens from their fellow men through the government's enforcement of the laws.

Both Montesquieu and Smith had a great impact upon the development in the United States. In her bicentennial celebrations, it seems proper to point out that the American Revolution, a continuation of the Whig revolution, was characterized by measure. Independence was declared on account of the excesses of monarchy. The Constitution was a reaction to democratic extremes. The founders' idea was free government, a popular government under which the majority, while ruling, for the sake of the individual was limited by a law which had to be strictly enforced. This was constitutionalism, to Hayek "The American Contribution."

Hayek, the liberal aristocrat, in recognition of the lawful principle, *in dubio pro reo,* with *noblesse* and in good scholarly fashion always has given his opponents the benefit of the doubt. He gave his works mottoes from that man of measure, Goethe. He addressed *The Road to Serfdom* "to the socialists of all parties"; perhaps when he addressed *The Constitution of Liberty* "to the unknown civilization that is growing in America," Hayek hoped that men would not lose measure and would again show the proper respect for the rule of law.

Antony Fisher

Must History Repeat Itself?

It is my purpose to provide convincing evidence:

1. That present world-wide developments are leading and will lead to disasters of unimaginable proportions; that these disasters will involve the death of countless millions from starvation, disease, and human slaughter; that these disasters, if they occur, will be the direct result of unsound economic decisions and are, therefore, inextricably interrelated.

2. That logic, history, and modern experience indicate that these evils can and must be avoided, but that the present situation is extremely dangerous. According to statistics compiled by the United Nations, out of forty countries whose rate of inflation exceeded 15 percent during the period 1968-1972, thirty-eight have in the meantime abandoned the rules of democracy in exchange for some military "junta" or other form of dictatorship.[1] History

---

1. Gunter Schmoulders, "The End of Full Employment" (Mont Pelerin Society, Paris, January 15-19, 1976).

tells us that on occasion after a disaster there have been almost instantaneous policy changes which have been followed by "economic miracles."

3. That since there is a way of saving the situation, it is up to us to do just that. The most significant testimonial to one of the world's greatest thinkers is not a statue, plaque, or memorial lecture. It is that his ideas should be put into practice, and this is especially so when the task would seem impossible. Ludwig von Mises dedicated his life to the cause of humanity, and gratitude is surely best expressed in action rather than words. Let me now endeavor to demonstrate how we can use his teachings for the achievement of good, perhaps as unimaginable as the evil which will occur if we fail.

History, theory, and modern experience, of all of which Mises had such a vast understanding, seem to provide us with evidence that history does not repeat itself, but that men make the same mistakes with the same consequences. Countless attempts to "share" wealth without an understanding of how it is created, inevitably produce the syndrome of inflation, ever rising taxes, ever more controls, "big government," compulsory "welfare" programs, food shortages, and starvation resulting in repression, civil war, distress, and mortality on a vast scale. In the early stages "the poor" do continue to benefit from the success of the market economy, and only suffer later when restrictive legislation produces inevitably its bad results. I call this repeated process "The Syndrome." These mistakes do not derive from the deliberate will of evil men to destroy their fellow humans—although on occasion this may appear to be so, as in our time with communist ideology—but from good intentions which themselves result from action based on "obvious" premises which are nevertheless incorrect.

For instance, some are poor and some are rich. It would seem therefore only too obvious that it is easy to make the poor rich by taking from the rich to give to the poor. The intention of helping the poor is so clearly a good one that it always has general support. The *method* is seldom questioned. But "helping the poor" in reality means giving them *more* choice, whereas the methods used, e.g. high taxes, controls, big government, result in reducing the choice of a whole community, including the poor. Unfortunately this last consequence is slow in revealing itself, by which time the choice-reducing process is usually out of hand, with shortages, high taxes, controls, and vicious punishments manifesting themselves without any obvious means of turning the situation around. The situation—the people—seem lost.

The remedy—taking from the rich—seems obvious, but it is a dangerous misconception. It leads to actions which are harmful because they hurt the very people they are intended to help. If in 1972 all private United Kingdom incomes over £5,000 ($8,000) after tax were confiscated, the incomes of the rest of the community would only be raised by 1 percent.[2] Of course the wealth producers would stop producing wealth as has often happened, for wealth production becomes impossible. Since cause and effect are not understood, further wrong action is taken which in turn produces worse consequences as the situation deteriorates.

---

2. Ljubo Sirc, "Is the Crisis of the 1970's Exclusively Monetary?" (Mont Pelerin Society, Paris, January 15-19, 1976).

It has been wisely said that "He who knows not and knows not that he knows not, is a fool; shun him: but he who knows not, and knows that he knows not, is wise; follow him." Of course it could be that the evils and disasters which have afflicted human beings throughout the millennia result from pure chance. But the evidence indicates otherwise and the teachings of Ludwig von Mises indicate a clear causal relationship:

> The interventionist interlude must come to an end because interventionism cannot lead to a permanent system of social organizations. The reason is threefold ... First: restrictive measures always restrict output and the amount of goods available for consumption .... Second: all the varieties of interference with the market phenomena not only fail to achieve the ends aimed at by their authors and supporters but bring about a state of affairs which—from the point of view of their authors' and advocates' valuations—is less desirable than the previous state of affairs which they were designed to alter .... Third: interventionism aims at confiscating the "surplus" of one part of the population and giving it to the other part. Once this surplus is exhausted by total confiscation, a further continuation of this policy is impossible .... [3]

The cause is bad government. The bad government has seldom received the blame. Groups and individuals have been blamed so that no correction has been possible.

Ben Rogge quotes Joseph Schumpeter as arguing that capitalism cannot survive, its very success producing conditions "which strongly point to socialism as heir-apparent" and "socialism" is surely, as I contend, a condition of such

---

3. Ludwig von Mises, *Human Action*, 3rd rev. ed., (Chicago: Henry Regnery Company, 1966), p. 858.

"reduced choice" as to cause starvation, misery, and terror.[4] Sylvester Petro provides his version of "The Syndrome" ending with his tenth point as "dissolution into the jungle."[5]

In my own book I contend that as "The Syndrome" develops the attacks on the individual "can ultimately reduce choice to zero . . . ."[6] This of course means misery, starvation, and death.

Are we all exaggerating? Are we dreaming? Are we having nightmares? One of the greatest men of all time, Aleksandr Solzhenitsyn would seem to indicate that we are not. "My friends, I am not going to tell you sweet words. The situation in the world is not just dangerous, it is not just threatening, it is catastrophic."[7] The *Christian Science Monitor* reports that India's suspension of civil rights has reduced by 40 percent the number of people in the world living in a democratic society—the worst decline in 25 years.[8]

All the evidence indicates that we are on that now notorious "Road to Serfdom" as explained so remarkably and prophetically over thirty years ago by that former student of Mises, another remarkable man and my mentor, Friedrich von Hayek.

---

4. Benjamin Rogge, "Will Capitalism Survive?" *Champions of Freedom Volume I*, ed. by Barbara J. Smith (Hillsdale, MI.: Hillsdale College Press, 1974), p. 26.

5. Sylvester Petro, "Labor-Service Agencies in a Free Society," *Champions of Freedom Volume I*, ed. by Barbara J. Smith (Hillsdale, MI.: Hillsdale College Press, 1974), p. 104.

6. Antony Fisher, *Must History Repeat Itself?* (Middlesex, England: Churchill Press Limited, 1974), p. 2.

7. Aleksandr Solzhenitsyn, "America: You Must Think About the World" (AFL-CIO, Washington, D.C., June 30, 1975).

8. "India's New Discipline" *Christian Science Monitor*, January 5, 1976, p. 32.

On occasion analogies can be helpful. Tie a dog to a tree with a long leash and a slip-knot round his neck and it is almost inevitable that the jerk he will feel at his first movement will frighten him. He will try to run. He can only run in one direction and that is round the tree. As he runs the knot will tighten and frighten him still more. At any moment he could stop running but he does not understand. The chances are that he will strangle himself against the tree.

Gavin Maxwell in his delightful story "A Ring of Bright Water" tells us how he kept his geese, near his crofter's cottage in Scotland, penned in during the night to protect them from the foxes. In the morning he would remove one side of the pen and they would fly away to feed all day and return at night. One morning he woke early and in the dark removed the side of the pen. Later in the day he found that the geese were still in the pen although there was nothing to prevent them from flying away. Only their ignorance kept them where they were. He had to demonstrate to them by closing the pen and opening it again in daylight that they were in fact free. Only their ignorance was their enemy.

Who has not seen some bird fly in through an open window and then nearly kill itself flying into the ceiling and walls of a room? Only its ignorance prevents it immediately flying out of the open window.

It is my purpose to indicate that the window is open. That the side of the pen is not there. That only panic resulting from ignorance is driving the world towards disaster. History does indicate that there have been periods of immense economic growth—economic "miracles"—but usually consequent upon sound policies formulated *after* some hideous disaster.

The disasters in every case appear to have arisen as a result of the deliberate minimizing of individual choice by government—Hayek's *Road to Serfdom*—until individual choice has too often been reduced to zero. Economic miracles on the other hand have occurred after the deliberate maximizing of individual choice. This would indicate that involuntary situations so created by government tend towards disaster and will produce disaster, whereas voluntary situations deliberately created so by government, have produced economic health and increasing prosperity for all, especially the poor. Mises' logic indicates that there is a causal relationship:

> The Market Economy is a social system of a division of labour and the private ownership of the means of production. Everybody acts on his own behalf: but everybodies' actions aim at the satisfaction of other peoples' needs as well as of the satisfaction of his own. Everybody in acting serves his fellow citizen. Everybody on the other hand is served by his fellow citizen. Everybody is both a means and an end in himself; an ultimate end for himself and a means to other people in their endeavours to attain their own ends.
>
> This system is steered by the market. The market directs the individual's activity into those channels in which he best serves the wants of his fellow men. There is in the operation of the market no compulsion and no coersion.[9]

Under these circumstances there certainly have been governments and there certainly have been laws, but the effect of the laws has been to maximize choice whereas

---

9. Ludwig von Mises, *Human Action*, 1st British Edition, (London: William Hodge and Company, 1949), p. 258.

during the build-up of the trouble, legislation has deliberately minimized choice.

How do we prevent an occurrence of all this evil? Solzhenitsyn tells us, "I understand, it's only human that persons living in prosperity have difficulty understanding the necessity of taking steps—here and now, in the state of prosperity— to defend themselves. That even in prosperity one must be on guard...."[10] That to me would appear to be the supreme problem. Who appreciates the real danger? Do I? Do you? If you do, are you making every possible endeavor to stave off disaster and turn it into an economic miracle? Without a supreme endeavor *to understand,* the indications are that we will go astray or be led astray. The communist machine is only too ready to help us go the wrong way.

In an attempt to aid in appreciating the dangers, let us take a quick look at three classic examples of human economic failure:

1. Can it not be said that the empire of Rome vanished into oblivion? There may be many opinions about why Rome came to grief and the measure of the disaster, but it does seem certain that the Roman republic prospered under legislation which protected the Roman citizen and his property over a wide and increasing area of what was then the civilized world. In due course "The Syndrome" developed. Government became bigger, the "bread and circuses" process began, the taxes rose ever higher, inflation destroyed the currency, the economy collapsed, and Rome became defenseless as the result of destructive

10. Aleksandr Solzhenitsyn, "Communism: A Legacy of Terror" (AFL-CIO, Washington, D.C., July 9, 1975).

internal policies. The barbarians may have overrun Rome but they did not destroy it. Rome destroyed herself.[11]

2. The French inflation of 1790-95 completely destroyed the French economy.[12] This period has been called the French Revolution. But a deliberate increase in the money supply starting in 1790 produced the inevitable increase in prices and the equally inevitable demands for price and wage controls. The clash between vicious inflation, that is a rapid drop in the value of money, and equally vicious laws attempting to fix prices and wages destroys an economy. All price signals are then hopelessly distorted, resulting in economic confusion and ultimate collapse. It divides the people against each other. The Greeks called this condition "stasis." Under such conditions nobody can live within the law and survive. In France the guillotine took its toll of the "culprits." The catastrophe was followed by Napoleon, who with his own wars, created further misery and death. It would appear to be the public who in their panic, like the dog leashed to the tree, actually demand the price and wage controls, as prices "rise," which if applied in a determined way, will destroy them.

3. The German inflation of 1922-23 destroyed the German economy. The inevitable consequence followed the same cause. But we face a serious problem in trying to be realistic, because accurate descriptions of what went on during these times seem so incredible and so far from today's experience in a free world. For instance in this comfortable auditorium I find it almost impossible to

11. Mises, *Human Action*, 3rd rev. ed., p. 767.
12. Andrew Dixon White, "Fiat Money Inflation in France" (Irvington-on-Hudson, NY: Foundation for Economic Education, Inc., 1959).

make the very point I wish to make, because in trying I seem to become incredible or at least irrelevant. Listen to this description of what happened in Germany during that inflation.

"In hyperinflation, a kilo of potatoes was worth, to some, more than the family silver: a leg of pork more than the grand piano. A prostitute in the family was better than an infant corpse; theft was preferable to starvation; warmth was finer than honour; clothing more essential than democracy, food more needed than freedom."[13]

Hitler was surely a consequence of this German economic disaster and he, like Napoleon, set out on wars which went a long way to destroying large parts of Europe.

So much for disasters without any awakening process. Let us now in contrast study three examples of similar catastrophies with a difference. On these occasions misguided governments with misguided policies produced disasters, but on these occasions another phenomenon developed after the debacle. A thinking process began which produced different policies and consequent economic "miracles."

1. The Mayflower arrived at Plymouth Rock in 1620. These Pilgrims made the "usual" mistakes and with the best intentions decided to own everything in "common," —choice minimized. After two years of inevitable misery and starvation they were forced into applying the market system with protection of private property—choice maximized. During the bad period they actually smooth-

---

13. Adam Fergusson, *When Money Dies* (London: William Kimber, 1975), p. 248.

ed over new graves to prevent the Indians from discovering the rate at which they were dying. The market economy was followed by an abundant harvest and for which the settlers gave thanks with a special meal. So that today when Americans celebrate Thanksgiving are they not doing more than thanking God for a good harvest? Are they not also giving thanks for a sound economy, or good government, for which purpose the Pilgrims left England?

2. How many Americans know of the devastating inflation of the late 1770s out of which crisis was born the American Constitution of 1789? This in turn was followed by a period of immense growth. Pelatiah Webster wrote at the time, "I do not mention these things from any pleasure I have in opening the wounds of my country or exposing its errors, but with the hope that our fatal mistakes may be a caution and a warning to future financiers who may live and act in any country which may happen to be in circumstances similar to ours at that time."[14] From this period comes the phrase "not worth a Continental." In his *History of the American Currency* the economist William Graham Sumner provides evidence of the absurd statements and misunderstandings of the time, misunderstandings so similar in our day and which are surely the cause of the trouble. He observes "that there is nothing new to be discovered about the operation of paper money. There is no new invention possible for making it 'as good as gold,' no new evidence conceivable for making it elastic, no difficulty connected with it

14. *In Brief* (Irvington on Hudson: Foundation for Economic Education, Vol. 5, No. 3. 1950).

which has not been experienced, no phenomenon for its development for which it had not abundant analogies . . . ."[15]

Again Pelatiah Webster tells us, "We have suffered more from this cause (the inflation and consequent controls) than from every other cause or calamity. It has *killed more men*, pervaded and corrupted the choicest interests of our country more, and done more injustice than even the arms and artifices of our enemy."[16] [Author's emphasis]

Instead of despairing, intelligent Americans proceeded to think out the American Constitution, probably the best document of its kind ever designed by man. It resulted in maximizing individual choice which in turn assured the effective and efficient calculating process so well explained by Mises. Among other important issues it would appear that it was also designed to ensure that the government should meet its debts on demand, in some form of final payment, rather than being permitted to reissue paper promises to pay. In that it has failed. Only governments can default on their payments for any length of time, but not even governments can do it indefinitely, as the lessons of inflation tell all too forcefully.

Mises describes the calculating process which requires stable money: "There are monetary units and there are measurable fiscal units of various economic goods and of many—but not all—services bought and sold. But the

_____

15. William G. Sumner, *The History of American Currency* (New York: Holt 1884), p. 326.
16. Sumner, *The History of American Currency*, p. 45.

exchange ratios which we have to deal with are permanently fluctuating. There is nothing constant and invariable in them. They defy any attempt to measure them . . . .

"We are not dealing at this point of our investigation with a problem of a 'quantitative science of economics' but with the analysis of the mental process performed by acting men in applying quantitative distinctions when planning conduct . . . ."[17] It is evident that in this calculating process it is vital to have a "sound currency" and equally evident that the United States as with every other country in varying degrees lacks that "sound currency." But decades of growth, the like of which the world had never previously experienced, followed the application of the Constitution and it is evident that this vast increase in wealth, which benefited the poor particularly, was causal and not just a coincidence.

3. A third example of the recovery process developed from the inflation and misery suffered by Germany after the 1939-1945 war. Dr. Ludwig Erhard stated that he was only able to re-establish a system of order because of the hopeless position in which Germany found itself. Erhard literally maximized choice with his bonfire of controls overnight in 1948. The vital cause and effect relationships which took place at this time must be understood. Many reasons are given for the German economic miracle, amongst them the huge financial aid given by the United States government. But the United Kingdom received almost equal sums. The difference between the two countries was that Germany followed Mises' approach, at

---

17. Mises, *Human Action*, 3rd rev. ed., p. 210.

least for a time, and the British government the Marxian
or choice-minimizing approach with higher and higher
taxes and bigger and bigger government and nationalization with consequent inflation, confusion, and approaching disaster. (Paradoxically the very success of the market economy, despite the onslaughts upon it, masks the
impending catastrophe.)

Now let me offer three yet different historical events
which would appear to teach still more useful lessons for us
at this time:

1. The first is that of the food shortages which threatened
   the United Kingdom in the early 1840s and which did
   produce a famine in Ireland. It would appear that the
   Free Traders under Cobden and Bright had campaigned
   so effectively and documented so thoroughly the potential dangers of high food tariffs, that when these tariffs
   threatened to produce dire consequences, a government
   committed to the restriction—that is, the government of Sir
   Robert Peel—altered its policy position, suddenly and
   radically bringing in Free Trade in 1846. Surely it was
   not surprising that this act was followed by a period of
   immense growth in the United Kingdom.

2. In 1964 the president of the British Board of Trade, Edward Heath, removed the regulations permitting resale
   price maintenance. He did this despite political opposition
   because turmoil at the retail level was being caused by
   the development of the new supermarket system. It so
   happens that the Institute of Economic Affairs[18] had

18. I created the I.E.A. in 1955 in London, on advice given to me
by Hayek in 1945. I produced its first publication in 1956. Henry
Hazlitt commented most favorably on it in *Newsweek* and copies
were soon sold out around the world. On January 1st '57 Ralph

published in London in 1960 a document on the subject which has subsequently gone into four editions, and which explains clearly the dangers of legislation permitting, with the support of law, the fixing of prices in the shops by manufacturers. It is apparent that this document was used by Heath. Instead of enforcing bad legislation which would have created worse difficulties at the retail level he removed the restrictive regulations and freed the market. This was done very rapidly in 1964.

3. In 1969 a British socialist government removed overnight the regulatory authority of the British Egg Marketing Board, including an enormous egg subsidy, which had been enacted by a British Conservative government in 1956. The egg market was in dire trouble as a result of the regulation which was harming the very producers it was designed to help. As always government intervention resulted in great misuse of resources at enormous additional costs. A fully documented warning of the consequences of the bad legislation and the great advantages of a free market was available to the Ministry of Agriculture. I had prepared this document myself and read it to the annual general meeting of the Poultry Industry Association at the end of 1967. I had been told, since the inception of the board in 1956, that "it was politically impossible" to get rid of it or the subsidy. In January of 1969 the government removed the board and the subsidy overnight on the advice of a commission set up to study the problem. "The politically impossible" had occurred. Time does not permit more details of this

Harris set up in a tiny office and since then with the help of Arthur Seldon has built the I.E.A. into a most prestigious academic center.

intriguing and instructive event. I use it as part of my case to indicate that if we are going to correct the present situation it is necessary to document what should be done now and the consequences of doing just that, as well as the likely consequences of what will happen if corrective changes are not made.

I must divert for one short moment. The removal of the Egg Marketing Board led me to hope that we might achieve the same ends with the Milk Marketing Board. The Institute of Economic Affairs published a study entitled "The Marketing of Milk" by Linda Whetstone in 1970 which achieved enormous publicity, as has a recent 1975 sequel. However, the Milk Marketing Board remains, possibly "saved" by the Common Agricultural Policy of the Common Market. I sent a copy of the 1970 study to Professor Mises, who made the following comment: "The essay 'The Marketing of Milk' by Linda Whetstone is precisely the kind of economic monograph that is badly needed in order to substitute a reasonable analysis of the economic conditions for the uncritical repetition of the complaints and wishes of various groups of people who are merely interested in the creation or preservation of conditions that further their own interest at the expense of the consumer," signed Ludwig von Mises. I quote the comment because it shows how valuable independent research can be. Too much so-called "research" fails because it is supporting some vested interest of business, politics, or most damaging of all, government. That Mises should have responded as he did was immensely appreciated by the author and all at the Institute of Economic Affairs. That Mises' comment was recorded at all is due to the very great thoughtfulness of Mrs. Mises and this gives me an opportunity to express once again my great personal gratitude to her.

Let me now sum up the lessons we have available as I see them:

1. That there is a basic principle fundamental to economic policy: that wealth is created at the fastest possible rate when individual choice is deliberately maximized.

2. That it must therefore be the purpose of government to plan to maximize choice.

3. That governments almost inevitably at some point begin minimizing choice in order to produce "wealth." This paradoxical act must produce the opposite results to those intended and will after a time end in devastation and too often has done so.

4. That the thinking process is seldom stimulated until it is too late. As Dr. Samuel Johnson once observed of an unfortunate man about to be hanged: "If you know you are going to be hanged in a fortnight it concentrates the mind wonderfully!"

5. For those with vision it is possible to influence the future by firmly staying outside "politics" and avoiding prejudice and all vested interests. Then by *documenting* the right course to be taken and the consequences which will follow, and also documenting the consequences which will follow from taking the wrong course, society can be spared the penalties that follow from minimized choice. The study and documentation of policy is in no way the same as taking part in politics—necessarily an exercise in party activity, so saturated in compromise and vested interest as inevitably to be damaging. At best, politics takes peoples' efforts and minds off doing more important things first.

There are several booby-trapped landmines in our way.
The first is the desire to rush into politics. The difference
between "policy" as such, and "politics" is seldom understood. When Hayek told me in 1945, as a result of my inquiry,
that if I wished to have any consequences, I must keep out
of politics, I think he may have been saying something
much more fundamental than he himself realized. I have
discovered that Socrates would have given me the same
instruction: ". . . He who will fight for the right, if he
would live even for a brief space, must have a private
station and not a public one."[19] I emphasize the need for
policy study, as this must come first. All the evidence
indicates that ideas do have consequences and are eventually reflected in political action.

The second landmine is the trade union problem. Trade
unions in many countries (not of course dictatorship countries like Russia) have been given too much power in law,
and this presents a real problem. The fuse which sets off
this particular landmine is inflation. Inflation plus impossible taxes on private income produce complicated circumstances which the Communists understand only too well.
"The confrontation" or fuse-point which follows is the
Greek *stasis*, which meant "the taking up of a distinct
position in the State with malicious intent towards another
party."[20] At the time of Wat Tyler's Rebellion in England
in 1381 the episode was described as "the malice of la-
bourers." They were resisting an attempt by government to
reduce their wages. Mary Lacy, writing in 1923 about the

19. *The Wisdom and Ideas of Plato*, ed. by Eugene Freeman and
David Arpel (Greenwich, Connecticut: Fawcett World, 1962) p. 22.
20. W. Ward Fowler, *City State of Greeks and Romans*, (London:
Macmillan, 1966), p. 250.

history of government attempts to limit prices, gives one consequence as "the dividing of the community into two hostile camps, one only of which considers that the government acts in its interests."[21] Could it not be argued that workers like anybody else forced into a position not of their own choosing endeavor to protect themselves?

The third landmine is the misconception that confrontation, or a crisis by itself, will automatically produce the right answer. As we have seen all too clearly the crisis does not necessarily produce the answer. Only intelligent premeditation and documentation can ensure that answer.

The fourth landmine is the assumption that the problem is only a monetary one. "Stop creating money by printing it and inflation will cease," they say. But they add that there will be massive unemployment as "deflation" takes place. They also point out that this is far better than hyper-inflation and here they are right because hyper-inflation is totally destructive. But surely this is only part of the story in our time. Certainly if governments are allowed to "manage" money at all they will mismanage it as regrettably as they must mismanage everything else, for they have no in-built fail-safe mechanism. But there is another problem to be solved if stability and maximum employment at rising real wages are to be achieved. The government must stop spending and creating money, but it *must also get out of all business and services*. Because it has no calculating process the government is only competent to make laws and not to offer services. There is today abun-

---

21. Mary G. Lacy, "Food Control During 46 Centuries: A Contribution to the History of Price Fixing" (Agricultural History Society, Washington, D.C., May 16, 1922).

dant evidence that nationalized industries are unbelievably expensive and inefficient, and this must include schooling (with its concomitant compulsion and bussing) and hospitals. Stability is required: not inflation, not deflation.

Let me offer another analogy. No pilot can fly his airplane "blind" in the dark without his instruments. Put the *best* pilot in an airplane without instruments in the dark and he must crash. The "climb and glide" indicator on the instrument panel may be analagous to the "profit and loss" motive, and the "turn and bank" indicator may be analagous to the price mechanism. These two instruments are as vital to decision making in flying an airplane as profits, losses, and prices are vital to the guiding of human action. Take a man away from these "instruments" or "direction indicators" and his human action must at least be wrong and probably disastrous however competent he may be. If the fail-safe type of mechanism is not available to those concerned with money they will overproduce it, because they will be relieved of the corrective process of having to pay on demand. That little-known but remarkable story of the inflation in the early 1800s of the British currency[22] indicates all too clearly that even completely honest and capable businessmen cannot make correct judgments about the money supply unless they are forced to do so by some automatic mechanism.

The fifth landmine is the mistake of trying to deal with that which appears *urgent*, and not therefore having time to deal with that which is vitally *important*. Surely if economic salvation depended only on a change in the party in power we should be in economic heaven already!

22. Sumner, *The History of American Currency*, appendix.

The sixth landmine is the inevitable temptation to offer "politically acceptable" solutions on a "for-the-time-being-basis." This temptation, if yielded to, means that no one will ever hear the truth, neither politician nor public. The truth, insofar as we try to understand and explain it, is that which is required for policy decision and nothing less.

So how do we involve ourselves in this non-political thinking and documentation process? The work of the Institute of Economic Affairs in London is now achieving consequences which indicate that this reasoning is correct. Reasoned unbiased documented evidence is producing consequences. Fear is forcing people to think and turn to the relatively few who have been talking sense—who have been right in their predictions—over a period of time. The fact that the newly-formed Fraser Institute in Vancouver, Canada, is having almost immediate similar effects would indicate that it is the idea that is working and not just chance or coincidence.[2][3]

Of the I. E. A. Patrick Hutber of the *Sunday Telegraph* writes: "Thank heavens for the Institute of Economic Affairs . . . what an incomparable debt we owe it . . . . It has become the leaven in the whole economic mass. The centre of useful economic activity is not to be found in the Treasury's economic section, not in the Bank of England, not presently in the universities, certainly not at the National Institute. More and more it is at Lord North Street,

---

23. 626 Bute Street, Vancouver, B.C. First Publication, "Rent Control—A Popular Paradox" is in its third printing since October 10, 1975. Nearly 6,000 copies have been sold, which is said to make it a Canadian "best seller."

the Institute's Headquarters."[24] And more recently on January 8th, 1976, Ronald Butt in *The Times* of London wrote: "The recent change of climate has been remarkable. Ten years ago the I. E. A. ... was still ... a bit of a joke .... Today, helped by the pressures of real life, it has shifted some of the best known economic writers in its direction and a good deal of the most influential economic thinking comes from economists published by the I. E. A. To most economists, the analysis of Hayek, Friedman, and other I. E. A. authors has taken on a new relevance—as it has to Chancellors and Shadow Chancellors . . . ." And on January 5th, 1976, Don McGillivray quotes Victor Hugo in respect of the Fraser Institute's activity: "Greater than the tread of mighty armies is an idea whose time has come," in the *Canadian Financial Times*, in a full page article.

Have I chilled your spine sufficiently, and does my advice about what to do seem convincing? If not, I hope you will correct me. Tell me where I am wrong. If I am right, how do we take this process further? Mises gives us this advice: "Everyone carries a part of society on his shoulders; no one is relieved of his responsibility by others. And no one can find a safe way out for himself if society is sweeping towards destruction. Everyone in his own interests must thrust himself vigorously into the intellectual battle. No one can stand aside with unconcern; the interests of everyone hang on the result. Whether he chooses or not, every man is drawn into the great historical struggle, the decisive battle into which our epoch has plunged us."[25]

24. Patrick Hutber, "Thank Heavens for the Institute of Economic Affairs . . ." *The Sunday Telegraph*, January 5, 1975, p. 23.
25. Ludwig von Mises, *Socialism*, trans. by K. Kahane, New Ed. (New Haven: Yale University Press, 1951), p. 515.

Those who cannot or will not think may "hide their heads in the sand." Others may try to build secret hideaways in such places as the Canadian Tundra, arming themselves with dried foods and bars of gold, but for anyone with any intelligence there is only one way. And what does that mean? It means thinking it through and, regrettably, thinking is the toughest endeavor to which man can apply himself.

One main factor in preventing the disaster must be to ensure that as many people as possible realize that disaster is inevitable if we continue on our present course. I will be told that that is impossible. I don't believe anything is impossible, provided we realize we need to do it; I myself have only recently come to this conclusion, that the warning process is absolutely vital, but that warning that the situation will deteriorate is not enough. We have to warn of the total consequence, document it historically and theoretically, and know that in the early stages that we shall be shunned as maniacs or fools. I have found in my own experience that whereas once no one would listen, that I was shunned, that I was asked to shut up, in the end when real trouble was just around the corner, someone did listen. In the case of eggs it was the Ministry of Agriculture who listened and the Egg Board and subsidy were abolished in favor of market solutions to people's problems.

What would the giants of the past teach us today? If the great James Madison were here what would he tell us? I venture to suggest that he would hand us a copy of the American Constitution probably pointing out that there were no alterations to its original spirit, but some clearer definitions, and even tighter restrictions on government discretion, especially in the field of money.

What would Adam Smith say if he were here with us? Probably he would hand us a copy of *The Wealth of Nations*, and draw our attention to the many passages which bear directly on our present situation.

And what would Mises tell us? He would, I am sure, say: "Do away *peremptorily* with all policies and measures destined to enhance prices above the height of the unhampered market. Do away with all this dismal stuff of price supports, parity prices, tariffs and quotas, intergovernmental commodity control agreements and so on. Abstain from increasing the quantity of money in circulation and from credit expansion, from all illusory attempts to lower the rate of interest and deficit spending. What we want is low prices."[26]

There was a time when rent control was removed in Los Angeles overnight. When R. P. M. was removed in England overnight. When the British Egg Marketing Board and the subsidy went overnight. When Erhard removed bookfuls of controls in Germany overnight. Our problem is not that of a drug addict. It is that of the bird which cannot see the open window but which is free to fly out of it. It is that of the prisoner in jail falsely convicted who is freed immediately. That there is an answer is a powerful boost to morale.

I am saying in its shortest form that the greatest event in the life of any one of us, of our community, of our nation, of our world, is that we should start thinking before the necessity arises. A voluntary thinking process is required. We must study cause and effect relationships, which are

---

26. Ludwig von Mises, *Planning for Freedom*, 2nd ed. (South Holland, Illinois: Libertarian Press, 1962), p. 184.

principles, and which affect our lives whether we understand them or whether we do not understand them. This in turn means trying to think without prejudice, emotion or vested interest; a striving for (mental) integrity, a striving for excellence. The alternative is to suffer and to die.

So we require a document outlining that which the government must announce now for action tomorrow. And what sort of document should that be?

Of course, we will be told that this is "politically impossible" and that no politician will ever put it through. But it has been done and a crisis has been the moment for doing it. Remember that our present course must lead to that crisis. Must we be so stupid that we once again wait for a crisis? Certainly not. And would the repeal of all this appalling legislation suddenly create mass unemployment? Erhard created ten million jobs in a short space of time. Certainly many people are misemployed and changes must take place, so we must free the people for immediate changes. I regret at this point that I do not have space to discuss moral principles. The evidence is that a sound economy is the expression of sound morals, and that in a free market people do tend to behave more correctly.

Bad government now as always harms the poor by lowering incomes with high direct and indirect taxes and by raising prices with inflation. By slowing or reducing national income it reduces earning and working opportunities.

In the United Kingdom a huge portion, some 17 percent of the working population, work for the central and local governments, not only producing no benefit, but interfering severely with the work of those who are productive. The market mechanism will sort things out extraordinarily quickly. It would be wise to set up a "golden bowler" scheme for civil servants, particularly in England, but even this may be unnecessary.

1. We must have an immediate repeal of all legislation which attempts to control or restrict free ownership or the value of a currency or foreign exchange.

2. The state must cease to have any role connected with money or the coinage.

3. All controls on prices, wages, interest rates, and other interference with the market mechanism by government must be removed.

4. If the collapse comes first, food must come before education, so that all schooling must find its own income from tomorrow morning. It will succeed in doing so. The cost of the equivalent schooling will be found to be much lower. As with all potential market developments many will say "impossible." Not at all. This is no more impossible than the development of the ball point pen, the pocket calculator, television, our steady supply of bread, and all the other developed marvels of the market economy and those yet to be developed and at this stage unimaginable.

5. All capital taxes must cease at midnight. Governments misuse money and they must therefore not be allowed to have one penny more than is absolutely necessary.

6. Since government expenditure will drop immediately, taxes can be cut immediately. All indirect taxes, particularly of the value added type, must be abolished overnight.

7. All legislation giving monopoly powers to any organization whatsoever, government or private, must be revoked at once.[27] The Government State Postal monopoly will necessarily disappear and not as in

England at present merely disintegrate. Something more effective will take its place.

8. All medical establishments will immediately set about raising their funds privately. They must be sold off or given away. They can be bought by private persons, charitable trusts, companies or non-profit making bodies. In England, means tests already exist and a simplified form could be used to protect people who may be unavoidably hurt. Not that the state must offer any service; with a means test and a voucher system it can care for those in genuine need.

9. All unnecessary ministries will be wound up forthwith. The Ministry of Health does no healing. The Ministry of Education does no teaching. The Ministry of Energy creates no power. And so on. Farcical ministries, such as those of sport and entertainment, will quickly vanish without trace.

10. All foreign aid will cease. "One world" government is not the way to peace and prosperity. Almost certainly it is wise to retire from such organizations as the United Nations, now becoming positively dangerous. The individual must be subject only to national law and courts and not to supranational law. The best of Magna Charta should apply.

11. Old age and other pensions are all in jeopardy as things stand. Under the new regime it will be necessary to phase out all state pensions in order that people should have pensions which will last them through their lives.

Neither space nor my understanding of the details permit

27. F. A. Hayek, *The Constitution of Liberty* (London: Routledge and Kegan Paul, 1960), p. 269.

more than this outline of those things which should be done *now*, many of which were done by Erhard overnight with magic effect.

The consequences of doing these things should also be understood. Immediately people will want to work, that is to serve, as Erhard proved. They will be able to keep their pay. Taxes will be low or nonexistent. The currency will strengthen immediately. People who think that their pay has risen in these last few years in those countries where there has been severe depreciation, as compared with those countries where there has been less depreciation, are still not aware of how much they have been cheated.

Immediately, enormous growth will benefit especially those at the bottom of the scale. Company profits and individual profits, that is real earnings, will rise rapidly. There will be continuing high and rising wages and employment. The "easy" life which leads to destruction will cease and a "harder" life leading to ever-better living standards will have recommenced.

The countries of the West adopting such a policy will suddenly find themselves strong in every respect and able to resist the wiles of the communist machine both internally and externally. There is nothing between us and this apparent heaven but our lack of understanding, which it is up to us to remedy right now.

May I conclude by asking, "have I at least gone some way in indicating our present course as one leading to disaster?" Let Solzhenitsyn lend force to my argument: "In its efforts to avoid the Third World War at all costs the West, in effect, allowed it to slip into the world . . . . The Third World War has already taken place and has ended in defeat .... Two or three decades of peaceful co-existence as glorious as the last three and the very concept of the West will disappear from the face of the earth."[28]

And he asks: "Is it then possible or impossible to transmit the experience of those who have suffered to those who have yet to suffer? Can one part of humanity learn from the bitter experience of another or can it not? Is it possible or impossible to warn someone of danger?"[29] We must answer YES and mean it. Mises confirms: "We stand on the brink of a precipice which threatens to engulf our civilization . . . ."[30] But of the possibilities of disaster he says: "I do not share this gloomy view. It may happen thus, but need not happen thus."[31]

I hope I have provided convincing evidence that there is a way out. In one sense it is an easy way out in that it requires our mental capacity. But in another sense, it is very diffcult because we all instinctively resist being made to think.

My case is that we *can* "make tomorrow" and therefore that we *must* make it a *good* tomorrow. History will indicate that it isn't even a case of millions of people doing a lot of intelligent thinking, it is enough if only a few will do so. It is up to each of us. It is up to me. It is up to you.

The way may not be obvious, but we get this encouragement from the book of Job. "There is a path which no

28. Aleksandr Solzhenitsyn, "The Third World War" *The Daily Telegraph Magazine*, August 8, 1975, p. 3.

29. Solzhenitsyn, *Communism.*

30. Mises, *Socialism*, p. 24.

31. Mises, *Socialism*, p. 23.

fowl knoweth, and which the vultures eye hath not seen." The path may be that difficult to find. But it is there. I hope I have shown the way. So let us take it, not next year, not next month, not next week, not tomorrow ... now.

Shirley R. Letwin

The Morality
of the Free Man

Of course we all believe in freedom; and we all believe in morality. But putting the two together is something of a problem. We think of morality as rather like the God of C. S. Lewis' schoolboy who said: "God is the sort of person who is always snooping around to see if anyone is enjoying himself and then trying to stop it." As freedom is the sort of person who would let us do what we like, a marriage between the two hardly promises to last.

The incompatibility of that marriage is especially embarrassing for those who defend freedom and also consider the restraints of morality essential to freedom. They can all too easily be disconcerted by the question: "If you believe in the importance of morality, why not advocate more and better regulation by government to turn us all into the best sort of men instead of agitating for freedom from regulation?"

These difficulties are more serious than they seem. They arise from trying to defend the wrong morality, one that really is not compatible with what we think of as freedom.

The morality that we are inclined to draw on when we defend discipline, order, and civilized standards is one that we have inherited from ancient, pagan philosophers. We have accepted it largely unwittingly because Christianity had early on become intertwined with ideas derived from pagan philosophers, which were irresistible because they made possible such comprehensive accounts of the human condition. It is only since the Reformation that the difficulties of accommodating Judeo-Christian beliefs to the fundamental pagan concepts on which Christian theology had been based, have been widely acknowledged. Nevertheless, Christians—along with atheists of all persuasions—continue to this day to think in a vocabulary drawn from this pagan morality.

It has taught us to see ourselves as unstable, precarious compounds of spirit and matter, divinity and brutishness, reason and passion. And moral perfection therefore seems to consist in securing the triumph of our higher rational or spiritual part over the lower, material, animal part.

What makes this sort of morality so troublesome for modern men in the West is that it conflicts with the aspiration that they have cultivated with a peculiar intensity—to have their individuality recognized and respected. This is the precise ambition imbedded in the loose talk about freedom that preoccupies the modern world. But in the pagan morality that these same modern men also espouse, individuality cannot be anything but a defect. It is a symptom of an incomplete spirituality or alienation from the spiritual, ruling principle of the cosmos. Individuality therefore becomes synonymous with barbarism and selfishness, and to the degree that men are perfected morally, they are expected to lose their individuality. It is hardly surprising that discerning and educated defenders of Western civilization have concluded that to cultivate morality we must renounce individuality, which they describe as egoism and self-interest. And on the other hand, those who do not enjoy the idea of becoming pure spirits feel obliged to renounce morality.

But there is available to us an alternative. It is not altogether unknown. It has not, however, been sharply distinguished from the other opposed morality that we have inherited. And the failure to recognize the antagonism between these moralities has produced moral and political muddle. We have carelessly drawn bits from each and assembled them in a collage that looks good enough until a searching question forces us to notice that the picture we made with our scissors and paste is only a jumble.

The alternative morality which we must learn to under-stand developed in England. It has sustained the political institutions for which England has been justly admired, and which the colonists in America so wisely took over and perfected, though sometimes by using alien words. These are what we think of as the political institutions of free men. But the morality underlying them grew up and was perpetuated unselfconsciously, and now that it has come under a concerted attack, even its most faithful practi-tioners do not know how to defend it. It can best be described as the "morality of the gentleman" because it is associated with that phenomenon which has long been recog-nized as England's greatest peculiarity.

The original meaning of gentleman was a "free" man as distinguished from a "freed" man or a serf. This meaning was gradually elaborated into an understanding of human conduct which can genuinely satisfy the aspirations of modern men to have their individuality fully respected. But a coherent and detailed exposition is only to be found in the conception of the gentleman's morality that runs through the English novelists, from Richardson and Fielding to Jane Austen and Trollope. This conception, however, remains entirely implicit in how characters are presented and judged.

I shall try to make explicit what these novelists took for granted by sketching the premises of their moral vocabulary. It is this vocabulary that we must deliberately relearn if we are to think coherently as free men and answer challenges from those who have no use for freedom. For unless we are clear about how free men understand their moral conduct, how a free man orders his private consciousness, our advocacy of certain institutions and policies will be a hollow affectation because it will lack any personal content.

The foundation of the gentleman's morality is his understanding of a human being as a concrete, unique, rational whole. This means that human beings are not supposed to consist of higher and lower parts. They are not souls imprisoned in bodies, or any other kind of adulterated spirit struggling for purification. A common way of summing up this view of human beings is by saying that each man has an immortal soul to look after. But the connotation often emphasized—that men are essentially spiritual—is foreign to the gentleman, and all the more so if he is Christian. For aspirations to spirituality belong to a pagan view of the universe which the gentleman rejects, and which has no room for men who aspire to individuality.

When the gentleman equates human beings with "immortal souls," he means that a man is not to be regarded as a part of a superior whole of any kind. A man is neither a fractured divinity nor an instance of a species; each individual is a species in himself. The special and equal worth of every man consists in his capacity to recognize himself as a being whose destiny belongs to himself alone. The immortality that he can aspire to is not that of a delinquent spirit restored to its original perfection but of an essentially mortal creature upon whom God may will to bestow eternal life after death.

This understanding of human beings was introduced by the Judeo-Christian religion. It is not exclusive to those who accept that religion. But it follows from seeing men as creatures of a God who is a Creator of all that is, who is the source of being and not just an ordering, rational principle. In the ancient, pagan cosmos, where the divinity is an ordering principle, not a Creator, men share in God's reason. But the creatures of the Judeo-Christian God enjoy no kinship with him. They were made out of nothing and inherited no part of God's nature. Men therefore have nothing in common with God. Their relationship to him cannot be based on likeness or knowledge, but only on faith, obedience, and love.

The implication of this picture of the universe is that the order of the universe can never become transparent to human reason because men cannot know how or why it came to be. Human life then is bounded by an impenetrable mystery. Human beings have no access to universal, necessary truth. But there are two compensations for cultivating such modesty which are crucial for men who care to be respected as individuals.

First, the Christian conception of a communion between men and a divinity who is a wholly alien, incomprehensible being introduced a revolutionary idea into Western civilization. It suggested that there can be a relationship which to pagan philosophers was incomprehensible. Christianity taught Europeans to conceive of a free association between separate beings who are not connected by likeness or knowledge of one another, and can never be reduced to a unity. This new kind of relationship has made it possible to suppose that human beings can associate with one another without overcoming or repressing their individuality.

Secondly, on this picture of a mysterious universe, the conflict between rationality and individuality vanishes. For reason acquires a new character. It is not a divine spark in men, but a purely human quality. Reason becomes a capacity to shape and transform human experience endlessly by creating new interpretations and responses. Instead of being an improving gloss of spirit over a base layer of passion or brutishness, reason necessarily permeates all the activities of every man in full possession of his faculties. There are no higher and lower parts to a man, and reason cannot be at war with any part of experience because reason constitutes all of experience.

Although every man has to eat in order to survive, his reason unavoidably confronts him with perceptions of alternative ways to do so—whether to hunt or to fish, whether just to fill his gut or to make an art of eating, whether to exert himself to survive or to choose death. Even if a man sets out to do just as the animals do, there are alternatives which he has rejected. And the possibilities discovered and chosen can be different for every man, not because of any defect or evil, but because even in an empty room, every man may interpret and respond to his experience differently. He can always discover another aspect or make a new connection. Far from conflicting with individuality, reason becomes the source of individuality.

What constitutes the human predicament in the gentleman's universe is the capacity that reason gives men for inventing new alternatives, combined with the impossibility of discovering limits to human imaginings outside of human life, because there mystery rules. For once nature loses its rationalist character, once nature no longer embodies a divine or rational ordering principle, it can only set conditions; it cannot provide a measure for right and wrong, or good and bad.

This means that all talk of natural rights or functions becomes meaningless in the gentleman's morality. In a way, the object of the gentleman's morality is like that of all other moralities—to discover some permanence in an existence where everything is ephemeral. But the permanence sought is of a very different sort. It is conquest of the ever changing uncertainty of human existence, not by renouncing, or trying to stop it or discovering a certainty outside of human life, but by developing a steady way of dealing with change.

This steadiness is what the gentleman calls "integrity." And it is the only sort of objective for moral conduct compatible with respecting individuality. In the traditional moralities, a well-ordered life is expected to bring fulfill-ment. Whether these moralities explicitly acknowledge an allegiance to a pagan metaphysics, or start from so-called common sense, they equate self-realization with fulfilling a hierarchy of capacities given by membership in a species, or a function in the social whole. But for men who are not parts of anything, fulfillment cannot be the measure for their lives. It is replaced by integrity.

A man may regard the obligation to achieve integrity as a trust given to him by God, or he may simply take it as the unquestionable postulate for his life. However he may come to revere integrity, what matters is that he is trying to achieve an order that is personal and not generic. It belongs ultimately to him alone. Consequently the effort to achieve integrity cannot oppose or in any way threaten individ-uality. Because a morality based on integrity can reconcile order with uniqueness, it is the morality of free men.

But integrity is far from easy to understand and not just because it is so easily confused with antagonistic traditional notions. While it is obvious that the word "integrity" suggests a kind of wholeness, what makes it peculiar is that it is a whole without parts or limits.

We can assign qualities to a man's integrity or give illustrations of it as when we describe his character. But just as when learning to see a painting we notice details in order to appreciate something beyond any of them, so integrity is a quality that transcends any characteristics. We cannot find integrity at the end of an analysis, make an inventory, produce a formula or a program for it. It is a unity that permeates and is displayed in all of a man's traits, but is not constituted by any of them. There are no parts to integrity.

Nor does integrity have any limits because it is a whole that is constantly changing. As it always belongs to a particular man, it has a finite frame and canvas, and yet these are not given or fixed limits because they are constantly being revised. One might describe integrity as a dramatic unity, not because it consists in playing certain roles or performing certain actions, but because it is a patterned movement.

Such a constantly moving unity is made possible by the connectedness of a man's thoughts and actions. This does not mean that everything is attached to a fixed center. The notion that we have a "core of personality" which is "always trying to break through the standardized public identity," as Lionel Trilling put it, makes no sense to the gentleman. For he does not understand himself as a fixed "nature" which is imposed upon, repressed or masked by some external force. His selfhood is always in the course of being produced by himself alone. Nevertheless a man of integrity does not suddenly see everything differently whenever he hears a new opinion. He is not at the beck and call of every voice because he has a regular manner of remembering, distinguishing, comparing, and reconciling. By finding his own way of accommodating to unending change, the gentleman achieves permanence without *rigor mortis.* He is adaptable without being flabby.

Although it may surprise those addicted to more traditional moralities, his veneration for his uniqueness and separateness makes it easier for the gentleman to live with others. For he does not identify individuality with isolation, or self-absorption, or competition. Although his integrity endows him with a will that is truly his own, he takes anyone who tries to be a law unto himself or thinks that he can will in a vacuum or create out of nothing to be a lunatic. The gentleman understands his way to lie in a life among other men, and to be necessarily dependent on them. And he sees no incompatibility between such dependence and his independence or self-sufficiency.

He thinks of himself as the fortunate heir to a rich, highly cultivated estate and he sees no cause to shun the marked paths or to quarrel with the guides who can show him the hidden perils. The gentleman knows that by behaving as if he were the first man out of Eden, he will succeed in becoming the last barbarian.

Since his head is not stocked with patterns to which the world is obliged to conform, nothing about himself or his circumstances strikes him as a deviation from some natural perfection. And this gives him a certain indifference to his liabilities. When he discovers that if he jumps from a window, he will fall not fly, he is not disposed to conclude that a malevolent power has put him under a spell which he must struggle to break. His misfortunes, no less than his endowments, are simply the stuff out of which he has to make his life.

He is fundamentally hopeful, but not because he believes that all is for the best in the best of all possible worlds. His hopefulness is due rather to a shrewd realism. The only certainty available to a man, he believes, is that neither the blessings nor the evils of today can last forever, or even seem quite so good or bad as they do today. Nothing is only what it seems now, and the consequences of actions are never just what was intended, both for better and worse. Despair is sinful because it displays an insolent certainty that confuses a human with an unchanging divine existence.

Heroic attempts are not ruled out. The man who grows dizzy when he looks down from a three-foot fence is not a likely candidate for stardom on the trapeze. But the gentleman would not condemn him for nevertheless making the attempt. Only he would expect the vertiginous hero to recognize how high he will have to climb, and that if he should fall, he might produce poetry but he will not become an instrument of justice by railing against the heavens, or even the circus managers.

Just as he sees no need to rebel in order to assert his individuality, so the gentleman does not feel obliged to conform in order to be civilized. For he does not interpret his civilized inheritance as a set of axioms from which he must deduce correct conclusions, or patterns which he must imitate, or goals that he must achieve. What others see as social constraints are for him a treasury of languages which enable him to order and express his thoughts and to communicate with others but that cannot tell him what to say. In short, the gentleman does not think that his life among other people imposes or supplies either a catechism or a set of directions for how to live. Instead the gentleman expects his life among other men to initiate him into practices. He expects his learning to take the form of an apprenticeship to those who are masters of the craft that he wishes to learn. He does not suppose that he can find it all in a do-it-yourself book because he wants to acquire more than a technique. He looks for the insight and judgment that will enable him to practice the craft imaginatively, in his own fashion, and this he can learn only from one who practices the craft, from a living teacher.

The mark of an educated man is the ability to use a language in an original fashion without distorting it, and to distinguish a fastidious delicacy from a pedantic correctness. In the same way, the art of living for the gentleman consists in seeing what fresh interpretations a practice allows without producing impudent barbarisms. The gentleman is a preserver and diligent student of inherited practices or traditions because he enjoys change and individuality.

Since the moral life for the gentleman takes the novel shape of trying to achieve permanence without escaping from or despising the transience of the human world, it is hardly surprising that the cardinal virtues for him are not the traditional ones. Even when they bear the same name they have a different meaning because they involve a different moral vocabulary. The postulates of this vocabulary of free men can be summed up in the four cardinal virtues of the gentleman: discrimination, diffidence, courage, and truthfulness.

The place given to wisdom in the traditional list is assigned by the gentleman to discrimination. Since his universe is not divided between an apparent diversity and a real unity, he takes no interest in the traditional exercise of reducing multiplicity to a common denominator, the ambition that led Thales to discover water, Marx to reveal the laws of history, and Levi-Strauss to unearth structures. The gentleman's concern is to see more accurately the real diversity in an apparent unity, to discriminate more nicely between similarities and differences.

This insistence on discriminating finely does not make the gentleman a votary of tolerance who always finds truth on both sides. On the contrary, the gentleman considers a blind addiction to tolerance a vice, and all the worse because it so easily passes for a virtue. The gentleman is not one to reject all rules because they ignore differences in circumstances, nor is he so eager to be flexible that he never takes a firm stand. His discrimination leads him to disdain any such travesty of appreciating the variety and contingency of human life.

Instead of disdaining rules, he is careful to distinguish different sorts of rules. He recognizes that whereas in the law, explicit clarity and firmness about the rules is more valuable than a confusing attempt to achieve perfect justice, in dealing with a friend, he is concerned to do what is uniquely right for that friend, which may require breaking rules that he would ordinarily keep. He distinguishes between crucial and important, significant and relevant, minor and trivial rules. When faced with a transgressor, he considers whether he is dealing with an eccentric, a ruffian, a villain, a rogue, a criminal, a scoundrel.

The gentleman does not refuse to criticize or condemn others, or feel obliged to find a truth hidden in every assertion. Instead he recognizes that if he rejects a friend's condemnation of someone as uncharitable, he is himself being uncharitable to his friend; if he is indulgent to the murderer, he is being indifferent to the fate of the victim; if he is too squeamish to consider the possibility of a conspiracy, he may hand his country over to armed bigotry. But he is careful to distinguish between base suspicion and reasonable doubt, between malice and error, between a dissent from his own opinions and a sign of evil. In short, the gentleman's discrimination is a command of a rich vocabulary of attitudes, styles, moods, tones, and expressions.

The second, and to some the most surprising, of the gentleman's virtues is his diffidence. It is not like the more traditional virtue of humility because it carries no connotation of unworthiness or inferiority. Diffidence is rather an unfailing, pervasive awareness of the limitations of all human reason, of even any number of human minds, and especially of one's own. The gentleman's diffidence follows from recognizing that he can never see all around his constantly changing world.

His diffidence prevents the gentleman from supposing that everything is or ought to be subject to his manipulation. Nothing could be more alien to him than the Baconian dream of constructing a "sure plan," or the pragmatist's belief that every word and action is an instrument for changing the world. The gentleman considers proposals for reconstructing the world to match some vision of perfection ridiculous, as well as dangerous. He can find satisfaction in contemplating the past and present; he is not driven to be constantly active for a new future.

His inhibitions about manipulating the world prevent the gentleman from accepting the common view of benevolence as a synonym for morality. The veneration for benevolence—for doing good, that is so widespread now, comes of seeing men as bundles of wants or interests, whose only options are either endlessly to pursue satisfactions for which other people can be but instruments or impediments, or else to sacrifice their own pleasure to that of others. The moral life for such men can only consist in a struggle between altruism and egoism, or self-sacrifice and selfishness. No such struggle afflicts, or can sanctify the gentleman. For he is not engaged in satisfying wants but in shaping a self, and he takes other men to be doing the same. His moral life is based on more complicated considerations. And self-sacrifice for its own sake is to him a sin, not a virtue, because it not only violates his own selfhood, which he is obliged to respect, but may besides impose on others who care about him.

The gentleman is skeptical of benevolence because he is so concerned about giving others—as individuals—their due. His awareness of the uniqueness and ultimate mystery of each person makes him cautious about the dangers of misunderstanding others. Of course it is unthinkable for him to help people in order to improve the species, or to serve humanity, or exercise his own virtue—to his way of thinking, all such efforts most flagrantly deny the humanity of his fellows. He also feels obliged to remember that treating another man as if he were incapable of running his own life may be the greatest of humiliations. Talk of human rights as a guide to benevolence strikes him as the rhetoric of a tyranny that sacrifices real human beings to abstract illusions. He recognizes how easily acting for others may do harm by mistaking or ignoring their peculiar characters and circumstances. In all these ways, the gentleman's diffidence inhibits him from imposing on others by a reckless indulgence in the pleasures of charity. He thinks that true benevolence must be highly discriminating.

Nor does he believe that generosity consists merely or even necessarily in giving more than is strictly due, but rather in remembering always that one's own conclusions about what is due may be wrong. He is consequently readier to forgive or withdraw than to insist, resent, and fight.

This does not, however, make the gentleman weak or indifferent. Though he never thinks that he always knows best, he is just as far from both the aloofness of someone who has lost interest in human concerns, and the meekness of one who embraces suffering. What makes the gentleman indifferent or resigned to what others, who aspire to godliness, regard as calamities, is his readiness to accept human existence just as it comes. His acceptance of his own unimportance, of the limitations of his powers, of the mystery, intricacy, and evanescence of everything saves the gentleman from being either shocked or distraught when men and things resist his will.

But the diffidence and the discrimination of the gentleman have to be sustained by courage, which is the third of his cardinal virtues. Without courage, the gentleman could not endure the special awareness which distinguishes his frame of mind, that no judgment can be certainly right, and that nevertheless he cannot be absolved from constantly judging. As he has no absolute truths to stand on, the gentleman needs courage in order to face the alternatives to his conclusions honestly. Having judged, he must have the strength to resist hostile voices. For in a world where nothing is fixed, every judgment is subject to doubt and there are unlimited grounds for criticizing the most judicious decisions. A man swayed by every harsh word will soon reduce his life to absurdity. As he can have no certainty that he is right, the gentleman must be able to remain steadfast when he knows that he might be wrong.

What distinguishes his courage from obstinacy or arrogance is the motive of his tenacity. It must be intended to sustain his judgment because he considers it the best judgment that he could make and not because he finds it the most comfortable or profitable to believe or defend. Therefore the gentleman must be able to compel himself to see things as they are and not as he would prefer them to be. Here as elsewhere, the gentleman's acceptance of the irremediable uncertainty of human life makes him a staunch realist.

The last of the gentleman's four cardinal virtues is truthfulness. It has, however, a totally untraditional character and importance in the gentleman's morality because of his assumption that human experience is incurably mutable and bounded by mystery, without any unquestionable truths to stand on. But though the peculiar importance of truthfulness for the gentleman is allied to his regard for individuality, he has no use for the sort of authenticity in which the self is supposed to be a kernel of unadulterated willfulness which must be protected against the distortions imposed by civilization. He venerates truthfulness because it is the only remedy against perpetual seasickness in a rocking world.

The gentleman's truthfulness requires something far more difficult than never telling a lie. It requires him never to betray himself nor to deceive others.

In order not to betray himself, a man's words must conform to his steady understanding of the world and of himself. If his words conform merely to his thoughts of the moment which may change tomorrow, his words are nothing more than true self-expression. Anyone who has only thoughts of the moment, who does not know himself and has no self to betray, who lacks a steady understanding cannot be truthful, even though he may never tell a lie.

In order not to deceive others, a man must notice with precision whom he is addressing, for what purpose, in what time and place. He cannot refuse to attend to the context of his utterances without betraying someone. Far from requiring a disregard for the contingent human world as Kant's categorical imperative does, the gentleman's truthfulness requires him always to discern and to take into account personal identities and peculiar circumstances. He is obliged to speak differently to friends, and to strangers, in private and in public, and speaking truthfully is never his only or necessarily overriding obligation. But his care for the concrete context of utterances must never degenerate into either a willful denial of objectivity or a presumptuous management of others. And as truthfulness depends on taking accurate account of the weight and limits of words, precision of language is at the heart of the gentleman's morality. That is one reason why a liberal education—which is supposed above all to teach one how to read, write, and speak so that every word counts—traditionally has been associated with gentlemanliness.

The new character of the gentleman's virtues makes him an equalitarian who accepts none of the compromises made by fashionable equalitarians. Unlike them, he rejects all appeals to "higher ends" such as "humanity" or "progress" for justifying using men as means. He is not a snob. His respect for men is independent of occupation, education, or status. Hereditary peerages among occupations, such as the professional equalitarians venerate, are not recognized by the gentleman. For he rejects the belief in a hierarchy of being ascending to pure spirit that makes it plausible to grade men according to their occupation, to place doctors above farmers, scientists above businessmen, professors above carpenters.

In the gentleman's world, no occupation in itself carries a connotation of inferiority because the quality of a man does not depend on his ability to transcend human existence, or to conform to some universal pattern, to become a spirit. What counts is how he conducts himself in his walk of life, whatever it may be, how clearly he perceives limitations and distinctions, how delicately he can appreciate and accommodate to others unlike himself, how accurately and steadily he judges the circumstances in which he moves and what is appropriate to himself. The depth, discrimination, and steadiness of a man's understanding of himself and his world decide his quality. The superior man may as easily be a farmer, a shoemaker, a brewer or a banker, as a mathematician, a dancer, a cook. He may have left school at ten or be an economist.

The value of education in the gentleman's world is as an initiation into more refined and varied ways of imagining and answering questions about one's world. In the gentleman's eye, no certificate can establish a man's quality, nor can a lack of knowledge disfigure him. But ignorance of where his knowledge ends will surely make him a pariah. The university graduate who is unaware of what he does not know will rank well below an illiterate who knows himself to be such. The shopkeeper may be more suspect than the schoolteacher because a shopkeeper can more easily succeed by treating others as objects to be mani-

pulated into buying more dearly or selling more cheaply.
But a shopkeeper who tries to serve his customers well will
rank higher than the academic who writes to get a promotion. In the gentleman's world, philosopher-kings can be
slavish, and tailors as gods among men.

The kind of equality that the gentleman cares about has
no more to do with what one owns than with what one
does for a living. Inequalities in income, rank, or achievement cannot injure the self-respect of the gentleman because that depends wholly on what he thinks of his behavior. To his mind, a man who supposes that his quality
rises and falls inversely with his neighbor's fortunes has
nothing to lose.

His awareness of the difference between men and gods
disposes the gentleman to recognize also that a mortal
being may wish to liberate himself from spending time and
energy on deciding some matters in order to devote himself
to others. Therefore the gentleman is as likely to consider
having some conditions of his life decided for him a privilege rather than a deprivation. That others may decide not
quite as he would have wished for him is but another
aspect of an existence in which almost everything will be
somewhat different from what one would like, and nevertheless may not be despicable. The gentleman would no
sooner equate self-respect with deciding everything in one's
life than try to fly by flapping his arms.

That a worker relies on others to organize the production in which he is engaged, or to provide him with materials and tools, cannot constitute a humiliation. It may be
an annoyance, but it may also be a liberation from responsibility and risk. What does matter for the gentleman is that

he can choose among different conditions of work, or can attempt to create such as are not available to him. But he always distinguishes between being dependent and being coerced, between an inability to do or acquire whatever he fancies and being used by others.

Thus the gentleman's morality offers us a coherent and precise understanding of what modern men have aspired to when they have talked of pursuing individuality and freedom. This way of seeing human life can explain how men can be associated without being alike or submissive, without being reduced to parts of a superior whole, but recognized as distinct, separate, and of equal worth. It allows us to accept the multiplicity and unpredictability of human life without feeling debased by it or pursuing destructive dreams. It shows us why we are not obliged to rebel against our civilized inheritance in order to assert our individuality.

And now we can answer the question: If we believe that moral excellence should be encouraged, why should we not use government to promote it? The answer in short is that what we understand by moral excellence is logically inconsistent with making laws to produce it. For it is a kind of excellence that does not consist in a set of goals which everyone ought to pursue, or a pattern to which all men should conform. It consists in each man's ability to make a coherent, self-sufficient life for himself in his own way among other men, while meticulously respecting the efforts of others to do the same.

Laws designed to produce such an achievement are a self-contradiction because what is intrinsically, and not just circumstantially, unique to each man cannot be subsumed under a rule. The kind of moral excellence to which free

men aspire must necessarily be hindered by a government
that acts as an enterprise for producing "the good life"
even if that is defined very abstractly as the fulfillment of
human potentialities in the right order. For such an objective implies that individual human beings are instances of a
species, not persons with unique destinies. To the degree
that individuals are treated by the government as means to
achieving a common substantive purpose, whatever its nature, their character as unique persons is deformed and
their pursuit of selfhood is thwarted.

Men who govern their conduct by the gentleman's morality think of their life with other men not as an enterprise
for achieving this or that but as a civil association. Such an
association has no substantive goals of any kind. It is
nothing like either a hospital or a school. It is not out to
produce more health or education or even wealth or good
citizens. Its purpose is to make rules for the communal life
of men who see themselves as unique persons, who want to
pursue their own projects, and wish to associate with others
who share this view.

Free men who live by the gentleman's morality do not
feel threatened by rules as such. They welcome them as one
of the resources for ordering their lives. It is the character
of the rules that concerns them above all. The kind of rules
that they expect from the government of a civil association
are ones that set conditions which all its members must
take into account when deciding how to run their lives.
What matters is that these rules should not degenerate into
directions or orders for what to do.

It is essential too, that these rules should not be decided
by balancing interests because the members of a civil asso-

ciation do not think of themselves as bundles of interests competing with one another.

Just which rules should be made must depend on what the men living in a particular time and place consider essential for preserving the communal life that they value. Of course a civil association will never welcome laws that direct men to do or think this rather than that. But they will expect some laws to discourage certain sorts of behavior, though the only legitimate ground for such a prohibition will always be that the behavior in question makes it impossible or unduly hazardous for other members of the association to pursue their private projects or to enjoy the kind of communal life they value.

It is conceivable that such laws might prohibit the sale of certain sorts of publications because those publications are considered "immoral." But the only ground for such a prohibition permissible in a civil association is that the sort of publication in question endangers or destroys respect for the rational individuality of each human being. What makes this a permissible ground is that commitment to such respect is the moral foundation of an association of free men who aspire to individuality. Whatever is designed to destroy this foundation may legitimately be considered a subject for prohibition. There may be strong reasons of another sort for rejecting any such prohibition by law—that the danger is trivial, doubtful or temporary; that the laws cannot be accurately framed or effectively enforced; are too costly, or will introduce dangers of another sort. But governmental action to protect the moral foundation of a civil association, understood as respect for the unique selfhood of each man, is in itself entirely compatible with the free man's morality.

Though it may be difficult to decide whether or how such action should be taken, that casts no doubt on the need to recognize such a moral commitment in an association of free men. Both the commitment and the difficulty of observing it follow from acknowledging that human beings can always interpret the same circumstances differently. Those who subscribe to the morality of free men accept this capacity as both their burden and their glory.